60 second solutions
MANAGEMENT

MANAGEMENT

GARY MCCLAIN, PHD
DEBORAH S. ROMAINE
ERIK SHERMAN
ERIC YAVERBAUM

David and Charles

A DAVID & CHARLES BOOK
Copyright © David & Charles Limited 2011

David & Charles is an F+W Media Inc. company
4700 East Galbraith Road
Cincinnati, OH 45236

First published in the UK in 2011

Text copyright © F+W Media Inc. 2011

The material in this book has been previously
published in *The Everything Managing People
Book 2nd Edition*, Gary McClain, Ph.D. and
Deborah S. Romaine, 2007, and *The Everything
Leadership Book 2nd Edition*, Eric Yaverbaum
and Erik Sherman, 2008, both published by
Adams Media.

F+W Media Inc. has asserted the right to be iden-
tified as author of this work in accordance with
the Copyright, Designs and Patents Act, 1988.

A catalogue record for this book is available from
the British Library.

ISBN-13: 978-1-4463-0048-0 paperback
ISBN-10: 1-4463-0048-X paperback

Printed in Finland by Bookwell
for David & Charles
Brunel House, Newton Abbot, Devon

Senior Acquisitions Editor: Freya Dangerfield
Desk Editor: Felicity Barr
Project Editor: Cheryl Brown
Proofreader: Nicola Hodgson
Design Manager: Sarah Clark
Production Controller: Bev Richardson

David & Charles publish high quality books on a
wide range of subjects.
For more great book ideas visit: www.rubooks.co.uk

CONTENTS

INTRODUCTION

'I have never been lost, but I will admit to being confused for several weeks.'
Daniel Boone

So, you're a manager. Congratulations! You probably have lots of ideas about how to do things differently – and better. Maybe you've already smoothly implemented some of them but have had less success with others. You know you could do more if you knew what to do and how to do it. Although you've had plenty of training in the skills that previous jobs have required, no one's really teaching you how to be a manager.

You've had your share of bad managers, and you don't want to become one of them. Perhaps you've been fortunate enough to have had a great manager at some point in your career; someone you'd like to be like now you're a manager yourself. We hope so, because that's the kind of manager we'd like you to be.

In today's business environment, success as a manager means directing and balancing multiple objectives. It's not enough to know processes; you must also know what motivates and supports the people who make those processes happen. This book offers you some tools to understanding how people function within the workplace and to figuring out how you as a manager can help them grow to be more productive and successful – so you will be, too.

IT'S NOT FOR EVERYONE

Not everyone is cut out to be a manager. Many who are at the top of their professions are among the worst when it comes to managing other people because that's not where their strengths lie. Only by being truthful with yourself can you know if you are one of these people. And remember, it doesn't mean that you're less valuable than those in management; a business needs all of its constituents to succeed.

management:
getting things done through others

THE SUPPORT OF YOUR STAFF

Although your job as manager may be new to you, having a manager is not new to the people who report to you. You're replacing someone else. Employees may be relieved and happy to see you in your new position, or they may be disgruntled and unhappy that the previous manager has gone. Whether you have come up through the ranks, or you are new to the company, there are many lessons to be learned, and fast.

What with balancing the demands of upper management and the needs of your employees, you may begin to feel as if part of your job description reads, 'Walk on water.' Don't worry – it's fine if your awkward sidestroke is what gets you to shore. It's okay to have limitations – everyone does. You can't do everything, and you can't be everything to everyone – no one can. What matters more is that you know your limits and can compensate for them.

WHEN YOU NEED A HELPING HAND

your promotion is real-life proof that they, too, have a shot at moving up the ladder

Those who excel in the skills of their jobs receive promotions to reward them for their abilities. The result is often managers who are not really people-people. They're skills-people. Are you a great accountant, programmer, sales representative, or production worker who has done so well in your job that you've been promoted to a management position? Are you feeling just a little bit uncomfortable with being in authority? Are you getting caught up in your own day-to-day responsibilities, still focused on doing a good job, and failing to recognize that managing means helping everyone else do a good job, too? Could you do with a helping hand?

it's not good enough for managers to be skills-people; they must be people-people too

HOW TO USE THIS BOOK

This book is structured so that each of the 60 solutions can be absorbed in just a minute or less. Use it as an active resource when you find that you could do with a little advice. If you are that rare person who is committed to taking proactive steps, you might be inclined to read the book sequentially. To derive its full benefits, however, keep this book nearby and flip through it to quickly find solutions that work for the problem you might be facing.

The 60 solutions are arranged in six themed sections. Part One outlines what a new manager has to deal with in the first few weeks of the job; Part Two covers some of the everyday duties you will need to undertake; Part Three deals with managing communications with your staff; Part Four focuses mainly on the setting of goals and priorities; Part Five looks at ways you can inspire others; and Part Six troubleshoots. Let *60 Second Solutions Management* guide you to become the best manager that you can be – one who can be respected, trusted, and maybe even loved by your employees.

not getting on with a manager is one of the most commonly cited reasons for leaving a job

part
one

part
one

UNDERSTAND YOUR ROLE

SOLUTION 1
KNOW WHAT'S EXPECTED OF YOU

'I know the price of success: dedication, hard work, and an unremitting devotion to the things you want to see happen.'
Frank Lloyd Wright

As an employee, you had a clear-cut definition of your role and responsibilities. The line around your job was easy for you and others to see, and it was obvious when your efforts went above and beyond the call of duty. As a manager, the 'and other duties as necessary' part of your job description will be at the core of your daily activities.

Although daunting to begin with, you will no doubt enjoy the diversity of your new role, once you establish exactly what is expected of you.

> *it's your job to help shape and deliver company standards and expectations to employees who not so long ago were your peers*

WHAT YOUR EMPLOYERS EXPECT OF YOU

As a manager, you are the face of the company. You represent upper management to your employees. You will be expected to:

- Reflect and support company goals and objectives, even if you don't agree with them.
- Reflect and support your company's policies and

procedures, even if you don't like them.

- Communicate the company's needs to employees.
- Give upper management feedback about how employees perceive and respond to company goals and policies.

A study by *'Entrepreneur'* magazine found that having managers they could respect topped the list of what employees want in their jobs. The survey concluded that the relationship employees have with their managers is a key factor in whether they stay or leave.

WHAT YOUR EMPLOYEES EXPECT OF YOU

Now that you are a manager, many employee expectations may strike you as unreasonable or unrealistic. Nevertheless, you will be expected to:

- Know what they want, even if they don't say anything.
- Understand that they have lives away from work that sometimes interfere with work.
- Pick up the slack when they don't complete tasks on time.
- Be available at any time of the day to answer questions and resolve problems.
- Help them acquire new skills, even if that means they will then become qualified for different jobs.
- Speak up for them when they have needs that require upper management decisions.
- Show your appreciation for the good work they do.
- Give them full credit for the department's successes and take full blame for the department's shortcomings.
- Remember that they are only human, but to never reveal this about yourself.

SOLUTION 2
KNOW WHICH HAT TO WEAR AND WHEN

'I am made all things to all men, that I might by all means save some.'
Corinthians 9:22

As a manager, the many roles that you may have to undertake could include friend, confidante, advocate, drill sergeant, counsellor, sage, and even enforcer, but your most important role is leader. Effective leadership means knowing which hat to wear and when.

you are expected to wear many hats and to know which one to wear for each circumstance

WHO ARE YOU TODAY?

Mentor - trusted guide Sharing the benefit of your experience with employees as they develop in their careers.

Teacher - imparting new skills Instructing employees in the expert knowledge they need to do their job to the best of their ability.

Parent - setting limits Establishing boundaries and organization at work, telling your employees what they can and cannot do.

Mediator - finding balance Helping people find common ground to resolve their differences.

Cheerleader - rallying the troops Motivating and encouraging staff to take on and complete new tasks and assignments, and believing in their ability to achieve even when others have their doubts.

Coach - bringing out the best in others Supporting employees either as individuals or as part of a team.

THE RESPONSIBILITIES OF YOUR ROLE

As a manager, it's up to you to be sure that you – and your department and the company – are doing everything possible to help an employee to be as successful as they can be. It's your responsibility to:

- Provide adequate and appropriate resources, including work space and equipment.
- Clearly articulate goals and priorities.
- Ensure that the job tasks are consistent with the employee's job description.
- Give clear instructions when tasks must be performed or completed in a certain way or by a specific time.
- Monitor workloads to be sure that an employee is working to capacity but is not overwhelmed.
- Communicate clearly and regularly with all employees to ensure they are working well together.
- Carefully document problems that you notice or that other employees bring to you, and meet with an employee as soon as you can clearly define these issues.
- Work collaboratively with the employee, and with their work colleagues if appropriate, to find mutually agreeable solutions when differences occur.

SOLUTION 3
CLEARING UP SOMEONE ELSE'S MESS

'Any change, even a change for the better, is always accompanied by drawbacks and discomforts.'
Arnold Bennett

Taking over from a bad manager is among the most difficult challenges you will face in your new role. All managers, even the bad, have loyal followers. It isn't necessary to treat these employees any differently, but it is vital for you to know who they are, because your first mission is to get everybody on board, and the loyalists will be the most resistant.

people forget how bad things really were, and they begin to reminisce about the good old times; before you know it, you become the bad guy

RESIST THE TEMPTATION
It may be tempting to turn your predecessor into the bad guy – by making him look bad, won't you look better? This is a risky strategy, as you may turn him into a martyr instead.

FIRST STEPS ON THE PATH TO GOOD MANAGEMENT
When you are replacing a manager who was bad by all accounts and standards, you have both a responsibility and an opportunity. Here are the basic steps to follow:

Hold a group meeting
- Express clear and concise goals and objectives; explain why these are important to each employee, to the department, and to the company.

- Ask for comments and thoughts; respond to negative expressions without judgement, saying 'Yes, that's an interesting point. We'll come back to that.'
- Respond directly but non-confrontationally to efforts to undermine your authority; if an employee persists, request that she meet with you after the meeting to discuss those concerns.

Hold individual meetings

- Meet with individuals to allow employees to express their personal feelings.
- Listen to what people are saying, and also to what they're not saying (see Solution 25).
- Question what doesn't make sense.

Present your improvement plan

- Give everyone a few days to think about and respond to the plan, then create a revised improvement plan that incorporates as many employee suggestions as possible.
- If you can't use a suggestion directly, use it indirectly and credit individuals for providing the impetus.

Build trust

- Continue talking with employees, both individually and in groups, as on ongoing process.
- Be consistent; if you change direction, have a good reason and present it to your employees.

QUICK FIX: FIRST GROUP MEETING

On your very first day, make the time to meet with the group to talk about what worked and what didn't, from a process perspective. Ask them to focus on workflow, assignments, goals, priorities and other issues related to productivity rather than personality – no finger pointing, please.

SOLUTION 4
TAKING OVER FROM A GOOD MANAGER

'Every new beginning comes from some other beginning's end.'
Seneca

What happens when the manager before you was almost superhuman? Are you worrying about how you fill your predecessor's shoes? Don't even try. The sooner you accept that it's not possible for a new manager to step in and maintain the same atmosphere that existed previously, the better. Each manager has different abilities, interests and priorities.

> *change doesn't inherently mean the end of good; it can mean a different kind of good*

ADDRESSING EMPLOYEE CONCERNS

Even when a change in management is desirable, employees might meet it with resistance. It's frightening and threatening to lose a manager. Even if the new manager is someone promoted from within the company, he or she is still an unknown. People may outwardly agree that the new manager offers new opportunities, but inwardly they feel worried. They want to know answers to questions like:

- What will happen as a result of the new arrangement?
- Will things be better or worse than they were before?
- What happens to former allies of a fired manager who still work in the department or work group?
- How will job descriptions and responsibilities change, if at all?

COMMUNICATION IS THE KEY TO SUCCESS

When you step into your new position as manager, good communication with your employees is essential. Here are some key points to keep in mind:

- Listen to employees so you know what concerns them, and talk with them so they know what concerns you.
- Confront the ghosts head-on: ask what employees liked about the previous manager's approach, and what they would change if they were in your shoes.
- Focus on processes, procedures and policies, not personalities.
- Refrain from presenting your views to change the world at the first staff meeting.
- Save your perspective for subsequent meetings, when you can temper your comments with the understanding that you have acquired from listening to employees' concerns and views.
- Do not comment about the previous manager's ways of doing things.
- Remain neutral and supportive of the company's goals; you are, above all, the face of the company.

QUICK FIX: AN OPEN-DOOR POLICY

As a good manager, employ an open-door policy; and, unless you are working on something that requires privacy, leave your door open! Most people see closed doors as stop signs; the only way people know you have an open-door policy is if your door is open.

SOLUTION 5
MOVING FROM PEER TO MANAGER

'Better the devil you know than the devil you don't.'
Proverb

Getting promoted within your work group is sometimes the greatest challenge you will face as a manager. Although managing your former colleagues can be difficult, you should not underestimate the advantages this gives you. You know what they like and don't like about the workplace, and about the management styles that direct and regulate the work they do.

you can afford to share the credit, as a good team happens only when there is a good team leader

THE FOUR 'R'S
You can help to make your transition from employee to manager go more smoothly by employing these four principles:

Resist the temptation to make immediate and dramatic changes Get a feel for what it's like to walk on the other side of the line first.

Review existing procedures and practices Meet with employees one-to-one or in small groups to ask them what they think works, and what doesn't, and why. What changes they would like to see?

Revise one step at a time Sometimes one small change makes a very big difference. Use a planned approach and review as you go. Incorporate suggestions from employees.

Recognize the contributions of your employees All work tasks require some level of collaboration, co-operation and teamwork.

HANDLING THE BUMPS

There is a chance that some of your former colleagues may feel resentment towards you when you give job assignments and evaluate job performance. The reactions of unhappy former work colleagues can include the following:

Passive-aggressive behaviour They seem to be going along with what you say but in reality are undermining your efforts. They do only and exactly what you tell them to do, not telling you when problems arise or when they know a particular approach won't work.

Anger They may be confrontational or give you the 'cold shoulder'.

Sabotage They may intentionally interfere with workflow – by 'losing' files or phone messages, for example.

Insubordination They may refuse to do the work you set them.

QUICK FIX: MANAGING DISSENT

Whether the dissenting behaviour is subtle or outright, often the most effective way to handle it is to talk with each offender individually. You can work out most grievances by giving your employees the opportunity to say what's on their minds. It is important to do this in private, as nothing fuels anger like an audience. Hear the person out before you begin speaking. Remember, most of what she is saying comes from an emotional base. Say what is necessary to keep the meeting focused on work, but do let her have her say.

SOLUTION 6
DEFINE A CLEAR PATH

'I'll go anywhere as long as it's forward.'
David Livingstone

Sometimes a manager steps into an existing work group or department that remains intact aside from its change of leadership. The employees are seasoned and knowledgeable, and passing the baton is a smooth transition.

When the previous manager has been fired, however, there are very likely to be productivity issues. Other employees might have been fired or transferred as well, leaving some positions vacant. Your mission is to rebuild.

after all is said and done, your key role is to craft a cohesive and productive work group

The sooner you define a clear path, the sooner employees can get on with their work lives. People recover more quickly when there is a plan in place that helps them move forward, towards new responsibilities and broadened abilities. You, their manager, are the one who can – and must – lead them.

A PERIOD OF ADJUSTMENT
While the public view tends to spotlight the people who lose their jobs in corporate shake-ups, these have also been traumatic events for the employees who remain. It can be just as distressing for the survivors as for those who have been let go.

People need time to assimilate and adjust. A good manager acknowledges feelings, and then helps employees to focus on the future.

MOVING ON

It is important to make sure employees understand their responsibilities, as well as those of the others. And it's essential to clearly articulate and support new goals and procedures. Ambiguity breeds mistrust.

The need to rebuild can arise from several circumstances. If market changes make it necessary for your company to revamp its product and service lines to meet changing customer demands, your job as manager is to identify the key strengths and abilities that existing employees offer and look for ways to fit them into the new structure. You will need to motivate employees to feel that they are valued contributors in the new order.

If your company has reorganized because of new ownership or to consolidate operations, the employees who remain may be suspicious and reluctant to support the new regime. This is fertile ground for resentment, distrust, anger and fear. You need to help your employees to identify the opportunities that the changes have created for them.

QUICK FIX: REBUILDING THE TEAM

The key to successfully rebuilding a fractured team is to communicate both with the group as a whole and with individual employees to:
- Clarify goals.
- Identify roles and responsibilities.
- Establish procedures for how people work together.
- Get acceptance and support from employees.

SOLUTION 7
IDENTIFY YOUR
MANAGEMENT STYLE

*'No matter where you go, you always
bring yourself along.'*
Popular saying

No matter what the situation, the goal or the other people involved, the one constant when you are a manager is you. You bring your history, psychology, strengths and weaknesses to bear to meet any challenges or demands. As you grapple with becoming a manager, your true self will always come through.

the more you understand how people perceive your actions in an impersonal way, the better you can evaluate how your leadership approach is working

If you want to be a really good manager, you must find out how your personal idiosyncrasies will affect your efforts.

Market researchers often ask people how they would react under given circumstances, such as whether they would buy a new type of product and how much they would pay. At the same time, they are aware that such data is among the least reliable. People often answer in a way that reflects how they would like to be thought of rather than what they would actually do.

TAKING A PERSONAL INVENTORY

You should be interested in understanding your leadership style so that you can use this knowledge to become a more effective manager. Now is the time to go through the Leadership Assessment Chart (Appendix A, page 152) and answer the questions as accurately as you can. Use this as a tool for active reflection. The whole point of completing the chart is to give you the opportunity to take stock in an honest manner. The more you know about how you approach leadership, the more you'll know about what tools and approaches will best fit your strengths and where you need to improve your efforts.

GETTING A PERSONAL EVALUATION

Taking stock of yourself is important, but it can be tricky. As human beings, we are deceptive creatures, both to others and to ourselves. Because leadership only happens in the presence of proper relationships with others, you will need to understand what drives those interactions. Make copies of the Reflective Leadership Evaluation Tool (Appendix B, page 156) and ask your employees to fill them out. The more you understand how people perceive your actions in an impersonal way, the better you can evaluate how your leadership approach is working. The results will help you become aware of the weaker areas that you need to improve as well as your strengths. Knowing both helps you create strategies to manage more effectively.

SOLUTION 8
ACCEPT YOU HAVE A LOT TO LEARN

'The only man who never makes a mistake is the man who never does anything.'
Theodore Roosevelt

As an employee, your outstanding job performance convinced your superiors that you were worthy of promotion. As a manager, you must demonstrate your ability to transcend daily details and visualize the bigger picture.

most managers learn about managing from the managers they have had through their careers

You probably went to college or university or studied on a training course or as an apprentice to learn what you know about your job. You relied on the expertise and the knowledge of others to show you the way to proficiency. As a new manager, you will need training too.

Most people learn about parenting from their parents and grandparents and from friends who became parents before them. They might learn methods that are ineffective, yet they lack the knowledge or insight to identify them as such. In the same way, most managers learn about managing from the managers they've had through their careers. They absorb the good, the bad and the ugly. Without a framework for understanding the intricacies of human relationships, they might perpetuate methods that are ineffective or even damaging.

WHAT MAKES A GOOD MANAGER?

Being the best at what you do doesn't necessarily qualify you to manage. It takes a very narrow, intense focus to excel as an employee – a dedicated, almost single-minded concentration to complete the tasks at hand. It takes a much broader, though equally intense, focus to excel as a manager. As a manager, you must manage a process, not produce a product. It's no longer your job to write computer programs or assemble components; it's now your job to manage the people who perform these tasks. You can't step in to rescue them when they become overwhelmed; instead, it's your job to find ways to help people help themselves.

as a manager, you must manage a process, not produce a product

QUICK FIX: MANAGEMENT TRAINING

Managers don't instinctively know how to manage. You should:

- Investigate if your company has a training program for new managers; if not, ask to be sent on management workshops.
- Enrol in management courses covering a wide range of topics, from legal issues to communication techniques.
- Ask a manager you respect for suggestions and advice – you might be able to 'shadow' this person.
- Browse the business shelves of your local bookshop for books on specific management methods or issues.

SOLUTION 9
LEAD BY EXAMPLE

'If your actions inspire others to dream more, learn more, do more and become more, you are a leader.'
John Quincy Adams

Managers set the tone for their work groups or their departments. Employees figure that if the manager acts a certain way, that is acceptable – if not expected – behaviour. You are what your employees may strive to become. Seeing yourself through their eyes, are you who you want to be? If not, remember that everyone is capable of change.

understand what makes people tick and know how to use that understanding to motivate and manage them

WHAT MESSAGES ARE YOU SENDING OUT?

Managers set the tone and the standards for attitudes towards workload, customers, the company and colleagues. If you start your workday 40 minutes late, take 2-hour lunches, and habitually arrive even just a few minutes late for meetings, you're letting your department know that timelines and schedules are arbitrary. If you do things when you get around to them, so will your employees. Conversely, if you're a workaholic who doesn't see a problem with taking home a couple of hours of work most evenings and going into the office for a few hours on the weekend, you risk establishing this as a performance standard among your employees.

BEHAVIOUR PATTERNS

People establish patterns of behaviour based on conformity. No one likes to be the odd one out. The department with one truly bad apple (or one outstanding performer) is rare; far more common is the work group bound together by mediocrity. If there are no incentives to complete work on time, nor any consequences for failing to do so, why bother? People need reinforcement to do the right things. Your job as a manager is to provide that reinforcement. For more on this, see Solution 23.

QUICK FIX: OBJECTIVE OBSERVATION

What if your employees consistently fail to meet your expectations? Try getting feedback on your interactions with your employees from a manager whom you trust. Ask them to casually observe you over a period of a week or so. Objective observation can reveal attitudes and behaviours that give messages counter to the ones you articulate. Once you can see yourself as others see you, you can shape your behaviours to reflect the attitudes you want to convey.

SOLUTION 10
LIFE IN THE MIDDLE

'The go-between wears out a thousand sandals.'
Japanese proverb

As a manager, you are not always a welcome presence in the workplace. Employees might resent you, often for reasons that have nothing to do with you personally. Even your superiors might be impatient with what they perceive to be your lack of progress when improvements take longer than expected. But you alone cannot make things work – you need the help and support of both subordinates and superiors to achieve the best for the company.

miracle worker is not among your many roles, although both subordinates and superiors might act as though it is

NO PLACE TO HIDE

If you feel as if all eyes are on you, you're probably right. As an employee, it was easier to blend into a crowd. As a manager, you're at the front of the class, and all your employees are watching you. Mostly they're looking for guidance (after all, this is your role), but they also want to see how you respond to challenges from both above and below. What

Some managers feel such a need for their employees to like them that they gossip with them, even going so far as to criticize the company. This is never a good idea. Employees soon begin to wonder what their managers say about them, and executives no longer trust gossiping managers to uphold the company's interests.

about your superiors, the managers or executives to whom you now report? Being closer to the top also means greater visibility. Frontline and mid-level managers are the movers and shakers in most companies. Mistakes at your level can be costly, with ramifications that echo throughout the company.

THE 'CLEAR VISION' BOUNDARY

Your role requires you to maintain a distance from both employees and upper management. Think of this as a 'clear vision' boundary that helps you to see both sides without becoming immersed in either. As 'middle' management, you can't belong to either side if you are to function effectively.

LIVING WITHIN YOUR LIMITATIONS

When you become a manager, your work life is no longer about you. It's about your bosses and your employees – what they need and want, and how you respond. Subordinates and superiors expect you to:

*   Know your own job inside out.
*   Know the jobs of your employees inside out.
*   Know what everyone needs, and provide it for them.
*   Maintain both motivation and discipline.
*   Enjoy coming to work in the morning more than you like leaving in the evening.

If you can't be everything to everyone, know your limitations and compensate for them.

SUMMARY: PART ONE
UNDERSTAND YOUR ROLE

01   **Know what's expected of you** Establish what your employees and bosses require of you, and enjoy the diversity of your new position.

02   **Know which hat to wear and when** Try out your many roles, including mentor, teacher, parent, mediator, cheerleader and coach.

03   **Clearing up someone else's mess** Make it your priority to get your staff on board with the changes.

04   **Taking over from a good manager** Don't try to fill your predecessor's shoes; focus instead on establishing your own management style.

05   **Moving from peer to manager** Managing your former colleagues gives you an advantage; after all, not so long ago you were one of the team.

06 **Define a clear path** Put a plan in place that helps staff to move forward, towards their new responsibilities.

07 **Identify your management style** Take a personal inventory and understand how your idiosyncrasies may affect your management style.

08 **Accept you have a lot to learn** You may need some training to become a better manager.

09 **Lead by example** Set the tone and the standards for your staff's attitudes towards workload, customers, the company and work colleagues.

10 **Life in the middle** Cultivate the support of both employees and upper management, but keep a healthy distance to ensure an objective view.

NOTES

part two

part two

MASTER THE DAILY TASKS

SOLUTION 11
BE SEEN TO BE PRESENT

'The problem with communication ... is the illusion that it has been accomplished.'
George Bernard Shaw

It is all too easy to come into work, go into your office, and be swamped by your emails and a heady round of back-to-back meetings. Before you know it, it's time to go home and you have gone the entire day without talking to the employees you manage, even though they surround you.

You must make it a point to go from office to office, and workstation to workstation to make contact with your employees each and every day.

> *consistent daily interaction promotes more than just good feelings – it also promotes effective and collaborative teamwork*

SMALL TALK MATTERS

When the manager takes a few moments to talk, employees feel better about coming to work and doing the job expected of them. When you stop to ask employees what they did over the weekend or to chat about how things are going with their children, employees feel that you care about them as people and as individuals, not just as cogs in the corporate machine. This is what helps to create bonds.

Ask each employee one question related to a personal interest and one work-related question. The first sign of progress is when your employee starts telling you about things that are going wrong, but you have hit your mark when she starts telling you about things that are going right.

THE ABSENT MANAGER

You can't know what is going on if you're not there. And if you're not there, people will attempt to resolve problems in their own ways, which might result in less-than-ideal results.

QUICK FIX: DOING THE ROUNDS

The daily round is a way of keeping in touch with the team, but beware, as there is a fine line between being interested and being intrusive, and it can be all too easy to offend unintentionally:

- Do ask questions and listen to the answers.
- Do walk around and listen to employees talk as they work.
- Don't sneak around – you don't want people to think you are spying on them.
- Don't hover – you want people to feel trusted to do their jobs without constant supervision.
- Don't miss anyone out – you don't want people to feel slighted or less important.
- Don't forget to go back – make sure you catch up with anyone who is missing later in the day.

SOLUTION 12
CREATING A
PRODUCTIVE WORKPLACE

*'We make the world we live in and shape
our own environment.'*
Orison Swett Marden

There's no doubt about it – what the workplace is like
as a physical and social environment is key to whether
employees are satisfied and content or dissatisfied and
stressed. The work environment needs to support the
tasks being done within it, and you should make it your
responsibility to make sure that it does.

UNDERSTANDING EMPLOYEE NEEDS

If you can ensure that the
working environment is
compatible with employee
needs and requests, the
likelihood is that your staff's
productivity and efficiency
will improve. If employees
spend a lot of time on the
telephone, or they need
quiet to help them con-
centrate, they may ben-
efit from office space with
walls that go to the ceiling

Marketeers use music to influence customers. Music with a hard, driving beat makes
people feel excited and impulsive, and
encourages them to make spontaneous pur-
chases and leave rather than linger – ideal
for fast-food restaurants. Soft, soothing music
makes people feel relaxed and thoughtful,
improving mental focus and muscle coordi-
nation, and encourages them to stay – ideal
for luxury restaurants, bookshops and expen-
sive boutiques. Would music be appropriate
in your workplace?

people spend more of their waking hours at work than anywhere else

and doors that close. If employees are working on projects that require them to discuss possibilities and brainstorm ideas, an open floor plan is probably better.

A HAPPY BALANCE

Most experts agree that it's important for employees to be able to personalize their work space. Many employees like to decorate their offices, work spaces or desks with family pictures and small personal items. Most companies find that this is not a problem as long as the decor doesn't interfere with job tasks and doesn't offend other employees or customers.

QUICK FIX: A SENSE OF FREEDOM

When people have too many rules, they either look for ways to break them or they leave. Whenever possible, you should:

- Allow some personal flexibility for start and end times for the working day.
- Permit employees to occasionally take an afternoon off or to come in late after working late the night before.
- Let staff schedule lunch breaks to accommodate relaxation activities, such as a stress-reducing yoga class.

SOLUTION 13
PRACTISE THE ART OF DELEGATION

'Many hands makes light work.'
Saying

When you were an employee, in the course of the workday you could accomplish numerous tasks and projects. You met people and learned processes that made it easier for you to do more with less, and you excelled. Now that you're a manager, you need to learn to let this approach go.

Your bosses expect you to delegate tasks and responsibilities to the employees who report to you. You are now the one making the assignments. Your job is to make sure other people get these done, not to do them yourself.

effective delegation is a craft many managers take an entire career to finally understand and master

LEARN TO DELEGATE

At first you may find delegation uncomfortable. After all, when you were an employee, you didn't much like it when the manager stopped by your desk to ask, 'Would you get these reports done by Wednesday? I need them for the project presentation.' Never mind that you were also working on the presentation – it was now your responsibility to do the reports too.

Sometimes it felt like the manager was dumping on you. Now you might feel that you're dumping on others, especially if you have come up from within their ranks.

STAY INVOLVED

When you delegate a task, even if you pass off an assignment entirely, you still remain accountable for its completion. It is important to set up a system that enables you to check that timely progress is being made without interfering. If you hover over the person you have assigned the job to, you will only succeed in frustrating and demoralizing them; and, for the time you are wasting, you might just as well be doing the job yourself. You must find a happy balance, and this will come from experience. You will begin to understand how to integrate the respective talents and abilities of your staff to get things done.

QUICK FIX: DECIDE TO DELEGATE

It may be time to brush up on your delegation skills if you find yourself saying yes to more than a couple of the following:

- Do you work longer hours than those you manage?
- Do you spend a large part of your day doing things for others which they could do for themselves?
- Do you have to take work home in the evening?
- Do you put off committing to social events because you may need to work at the weekend?
- Do you do certain tasks because you enjoy them even though someone else could do them just as well?

SOLUTION 14
RECRUITING THE RIGHT PEOPLE

'The closest to perfection a person ever comes is when he fills out a job application form.'
Stanley J. Randall

Finding and hiring the right people for the job is one of the manager's most important day-to-day tasks. There has to be a happy medium between finding the best person to advance the interests of the company and to be a positive fit in the group. So how do you find the best people for the job?

FINDING THE IDEAL CANDIDATE

Many managers overlook the most highly qualified candidates – current employees. Is the perfect candidate for your job someone in another job in the company whose shoes would be hard to fill? Discuss transitional measures with the other manager. Sometimes passing over an employee for a new position because she is exceptionally good at her current job is just the reason she needs to take her talents to the competition. If there isn't a suitable home-grown candidate, consider:

- Personal referrals.
- Employment agencies.
- Local or national newspaper ads.
- Social networking internet sites.

> Studies suggest that hiring and promoting from within is more successful than bringing in outside candidates. Yet companies are twice as likely to look beyond their current employees when new jobs become available.

THE JOB DESCRIPTION

A written job description defines the basic expectations that you and your company have for employee performance. This message runs consistently through advertising, interviews and performance evaluations. A job's specifications should be reasonable and realistic, yet they should also allow for expansion and growth as circumstances change within your company and the industry.

When written correctly, the job description is the platform for the job's measurable standards. The more effectively you establish this in the job interview, the greater clarity new employees will have about your expectations.

Most jobs actually have two sets of requirements: those related to expertise and experience, and those related to personality and work style. Requirements related to skill sets appear to be fairly clear-cut and easy to establish. When recruiting someone to operate a punch press in the production department, it's easy enough to determine whether an applicant has the knowledge and skill to do this. If hiring to fill a position in the sales department, the situation is far more subjective. Because the job involves forming short-lived relationships, work style and personality are significant factors.

QUICK FIX: SELECTING APPLICANTS TO INTERVIEW

If the response to a job ad is overwhelming, get the personnel department to review the applications, forwarding on to you only those that meet the job's technical qualifications and the company's basic requirements.

SOLUTION 15
PERFECTING YOUR INTERVIEW TECHNIQUE

'Do not mind anything that anyone tells you about anyone else. Judge everyone and everything for yourself.'
Henry James

The job interview is your opportunity to meet the applicants and ask questions about their qualifications. Just as the interviewer is assessing whether the applicant is a good fit for the job, the department and the company, the applicant is evaluating those same factors too.

one-third of job candidates lie about their experience, education or employment history on their applications or CVs

Interviewing is a craft. You won't excel at it right away, but you can become quite skilled as your experience grows.

INTERVIEW BASICS FROM START TO FINISH
In an interview you should:

Describe the actual job activities Explain what a typical day is like and what kinds of successes and challenges employees encounter.

Describe the work environment Is it collaborative or independent?

Ask a few questions that require simple, factual responses Watch out for hesitancy or for answers that don't match the job application or CV.

Ask for examples that demonstrate abilities and skills in particular areas Ask the applicant to describe two or three similar experiences that relate to the job description.

Press for specifics Just how, exactly, was the applicant's previous experience 'like' the requirements of the job?

Look out for unsubstantiated claims of expertise Always press for specifics and ask for examples.

NEXT STEPS

Concluding the interview Let the candidate know when she might next hear from you, your timeline for filling the position, and whether to anticipate another round of interviews.

Keep your thoughts to yourself Never give a candidate the impression that you intend to hire her, whether you do or not.

Take up references No matter how well a candidate interviews, always check references to verify the facts she has put on the job application.

Make an offer Telephone your first choice to offer the job. You're enthusiastic and excited, so let it show. Review the terms and give a time period for her to consider your offer – 48 hours is reasonable. Call back promptly and, if the job offer is accepted, send a confirmation letter by post.

If your first-choice candidate declines Find out why; there may be a chance to get her to reconsider. If not, move on to your second choice.

QUICK FIX: OPEN-ENDED QUESTIONS

When interviewing, the standard advice is always to ask open-ended questions to avoid monosyllabic yes or no answers. But creating open-ended questions is harder than you might think. If you are stuck, here is a trick. Instead of starting a question with a verb, use an interrogative:

- Who?
- What?
- Which?
- Where?
- When?
- Why?
- How?

SOLUTION 16
WHAT IS A TEAM?

'Teamwork is the fuel that allows common people to attain uncommon results.'
Andrew Carnegie

A work group exists because a company hires a number of people to perform specific tasks and jobs. A team develops when those people work together in ways that enhance their efficiency and productivity. As a manager, it is your responsibility to create such teams. Creating an effective work group is part planning and part luck.

Just as mixing chemicals produces different results depending on the substances and their quantities, combining personalities and work styles results in varied effects. Indeed, we often talk about the 'chemistry' among group members as critical to the group's success.

Changing just one member often alters the group far beyond that one member's role and responsibilities.

As much as we'd like to think professionalism transcends personality, the reality is that people who like each other get along better. A team whose members provide complementary skills can function competently and even productively without friendship to bond them. But when team members consider themselves friends as well as colleagues, they have a heightened investment in the team's activities. For more on building effective teams, see Solution 34.

EFFECTIVE TEAMS

Individual personalities and work styles significantly influence the team's collective identity. The most effective teams contain complementary, if not necessarily similar, personalities and work styles. Each person's strengths overlap the others' weaknesses. For more on building an effective team, see Solution 34.

> **team:**
> a group of people who work together to accomplish something beyond their individual self-interests

WHEN A GROUP OF EMPLOYEES BECOMES A TEAM

A team isn't a collection of people simply following orders. To function, a team needs the following:

Purpose A clear sense of mission and a reason for existence that answers the questions: 'Why are we here? Why is it us? Why now?' As manager, you need to communicate the vision to the team and identify their goals.

Commitment As purpose is related to vision, commitment is related to motivation. Team members must commit to undertake their tasks and to see the purpose of the team through to completion.

Rules of operation Team members need to establish methods of interacting, being productive and resolving conflict. For example, they may meet on a certain day and time each week.

Interdependence Team members must look out not only for themselves but for how other members of the team are doing. It's the entire team that succeeds or fails.

SOLUTION 17
MEET OUT OF NEED, NOT OUT OF HABIT

'Meetings are indispensable when you don't want to do anything.'
John Kenneth Galbraith

No doubt you have spent too many hours in meetings for no perceptibly useful reason. But to write them off as nothing but collective time wasted would be unfair. When conducted properly, they are an important part of a communication strategy and an effective way to work with team members.

the leading complaint in most organizations is that there are too many meetings

The mistake made by many managers is to hold meetings because they are 'supposed to'. If you don't need to have a meeting, or if the meeting will not achieve something more easily and efficiently than another activity, simply don't have it. If you decide a meeting is necessary, Solution 18 gives lots of tips for organizing an effective one.

Companies devote considerable resources to meetings. The typical manager spends at least eight hours a week in meetings – a full working day. Studies suggest companies may spend 10 per cent or more of their budgets on meetings.

TYPES OF MEETING

There are distinctly different types of meeting, and each can have its own requirements; it is important to understand the distinctions if you are to achieve your aims.

Brainstorming meeting Idea generation, often through a facilitator. Follow-up is key and an additional meeting may be required to decide which ideas merit implementation.

Work meeting When specific tasks need to be achieved, a focused agenda is important to prevent the meeting from dragging on.

Review meeting When assembling to go over previously completed work, it is essential to get material to attendees well in advance to maximize participation and moving on to the next step.

Status meeting This type of meeting is often unnecessary; it can usually be replaced with a memo or a report.

Start-up meeting This is the initial meeting on a project and is an opportunity to outline roles and responsibilities for a smooth working relationship. The attendee list is critical.

Regular or standing meeting Often pointless, particularly if selected participants merely take turns reciting information from printed reports.

QUICK FIX: VIRTUAL MEETINGS
Audio teleconferencing, video teleconferencing and web-hosted meetings are worth considering when you have employees in remote locations. They enable people to communicate without wasting time travelling to meeting venues.

SOLUTION 18
GET THE MOST OUT OF MEETINGS

'Good things, when short, are twice as good.'
Baltasar Gracián

Meetings can be interesting, useful and productive. Making them so is not only possible, it's your responsibility. All it takes is a little planning and organization to make a meeting go smoothly.

if there is no clear reason for a meeting, don't schedule one

AVOID COMMON MISTAKES

If you are going to use meetings effectively you must avoid the potential danger areas.

Too little preparation How often have you walked into a meeting only to get a packet of information that you are expected to speed-read and instantly understand?

No focus All too often there is no clear agenda or objective, and people are allowed to drone on, drifting from one irrelevant topic to the next.

Too little follow-up

Everyone is frustrated when things are allowed to drift, when there is no meeting summary or follow-through on assigned actions, or evaluation.

The administrative department at a large corporation resolved the problem of having daily staff meetings drag on by holding 'standing meetings' in which participants stood up for its duration. Discussions were brief and decisions were prompt.

MAKING MEETINGS GOOD

If you want meetings to work, you need to focus on getting the elements right before, during and after.

Proper preparation Distribute a detailed agenda in advance in sufficient time for attendees to raise questions.

Start on time Begin the discussions whether all attendees have arrived or not – next time they won't be late.

Keep the discussion on track Stick to the agenda; if important off-track issues are raised, make a note to follow up later.

Keep meetings to time Ten minutes or so before the meeting is scheduled to end, begin to draw the meeting to a close, reviewing and recapping key points, and agreeing follow-up steps. For more on meeting follow-up, see Solution 19.

QUICK FIX: MEETING AGENDA

The agenda helps attendees prepare for a meeting, and it forces you to more thoroughly consider what you want to achieve. Keep the agenda to no more than five topics and outline each in no more than two sentences. If necessary, attach a separate discussion page that provides the detail you want people to know. Identify the discussion time for each agenda item. Make sure the agenda answers the following:

- Where, when and how long is it?
- Who is calling it?
- Who is attending it?
- What is the subject of it?
- What are the topics for discussion?

SOLUTION 19
ALWAYS FOLLOW UP ON MEETINGS

'I think they should consider giving Oscars for meetings ... Best Supporting Meeting, Best Meeting Based on Material from Another Meeting.'
William Goldman

By following the advice in Solution 18, you will be on your way to running effective meetings. However, a meeting can only be judged a success once the actions agreed there have been followed up. Make sure you have an effective system for capturing, summarizing and assigning action items to the appropriate individuals or teams. You also need to follow through to make sure the decisions recorded have been acted upon.

for people to ignore what they agreed to do in a meeting is to waste the time of everyone who attended

Assign a meeting documenter – someone whose responsibility it is to record everything of importance

QUICK FIX: COMPLEX MEETINGS

For particularly complex discussions, consider having two document-ers, each taking notes independently. This gives you a better chance of capturing all the pertinent information. Combine the two sets of notes into one set of minutes before distributing.

and to make the notes (also known as the minutes) available after the meeting. The documenter should work with a copy of the agenda to hand, so notes can refer to sections of the meeting.

FOLLOW-THROUGH

Aim to distribute the minutes within 24 hours of the meeting. The more time that passes between the meeting and the distribution of the notes, the less relevant they will seem. If any of the points raised at the meeting require further actions, ensure it is clear who is responsible for following up on these, and set deadlines for when this needs to be done by.

Keep a check on the progress of any action points. Make sure employees have the resources and information they require. Do you need to pave the way for interaction with another department? Do employees need your help to access information or data?

A couple of weeks after the original meeting, consider issuing a follow-up document to record what was promised, what happened, and what is still outstanding. Schedule a follow-up meeting if necessary.

People like to know what happened as a result of their discussion and input, so do make sure you communicate the outcomes of implemented changes and solutions, either through memos or emails. Most importantly, thank people for their suggestions and participation.

QUICK FIX: BETTER MEETINGS
If you want to learn how to run better meetings, you need to hear from the attendees how they think things went. What worked? What didn't? The more you can learn, the more you can improve future meetings.

SOLUTION 20
THE ULTIMATE RESPONSIBILITY LIES WITH YOU

'On my desk I have a motto which says "The Buck Stops Here"'
President Harry S. Truman

As an employee, you were responsible for completing job tasks and work projects. Your manager delegated to you, and you carried out the assignment, but it was your manager who was accountable for how well you did your work. When you succeeded, your manager got the credit, and when you failed, your manager took the blame.

when things go well, share the glory with your employees

Now that you're a manager, you have the authority to assign tasks and actions to the employees who report to you, but you also accept accountability for their performance.

The manager who is setting himself up to fail is the one who has an over-inflated sense of his own importance. He feels important, he acts important, and most of the time, he rushes around looking important – much too important to engage with his employees. He stays in his office, behind closed doors, doing very important things, emerging only when he needs something important or to brag about the very important things he has achieved (all on his own, of course!).

THE POSITIVE SIDE OF ACCOUNTABILITY

accountability:
the acknowledgement and assumption of responsibility for actions and decisions

The common perception is that accountability is related to negative consequences, the fall-out from circumstances that go awry. But accountability also encompasses the positive consequences. When a project comes through and accomplishes its objectives, as its manager you are the first to receive accolades. When things do go wrong, it's more effective and productive to look at the circumstance as an opportunity for learning for both your employees and for you. How you handle responsibility and accountability is often the single most important aspect of your position as manager and the key to your future success in management.

QUICK FIX: THE FRESH START

When it becomes necessary to resolve a problem with an employee who reports to you, always offer the opportunity for a fresh start. The person should not feel compelled to continue a certain pattern of behaviour. No matter the trail of angry words that follow them into your office, let it stay at the threshold. This lessens the pull of past behaviour (however immediate that past is) and allows you to start over again.

SUMMARY: PART TWO
MASTER THE DAILY TASKS

11   **Be seen to be present** Make it a point to make contact with your employees every day.

12   **Creating a productive workplace** Make it your responsibility to make sure that the work environment supports the tasks being done there.

13   **Practise the art of delegation** Delegate tasks and responsibilities to the employees who report to you to.

14   **Recruiting the right people** Balance finding the best person to advance the interests of the company with someone who will be a positive fit in the team.

15   **Perfecting your interview technique** Take the time to hone the skills that help you to assess if a job applicant is a good fit for the company.

16 **What is a team?** Group together your staff members so that they work together in ways that enhance their efficiency and productivity.

17 **Meet out of need, not out of habit** Do not hold meetings because you are supposed to, but because you have something to communicate.

18 **Get the most out of meetings** Make meetings interesting, useful and productive.

19 **Always follow up on meetings** A meeting is only successful once actions agreed upon have been completed.

20 **The ultimate responsibility lies with you** You are accountable for your team's successes and failures.

NOTES

part
three

part
three

GET HEARD AND LISTEN

SOLUTION 21
RALLYING THE TROOPS

'To lead people walk behind them.'
Lao Tzu

You have been promoted to manager because you are a brilliant performer, but what will keep you there is how well you can motivate your staff and keep them performing to the best of their abilities.

show your team that you believe in its ability to succeed

Your employees may worry that they may not be able to complete the tasks assigned to them, and you need to help them believe in themselves. Even when your superiors are unhappy with their productivity, you need to cheer them on.

SHOW THEM YOU CARE

Your staff need to know you truly care – not just about their assignments and how they can meet the department's goals, but about them as people. Show them you do by talking to them every day (see Solution 11).

At sporting events, the cheerleaders always interact with the crowd, no matter what is happening on the field. They're chanting, dancing and smiling, working to stay engaged with the spectators. Their mission is to create a roar of support beyond what they themselves can generate to motivate the players to give the proverbial 110 per cent. Even when the crowd boos, the players know that the cheerleaders will still be there, cheering them on.

SOLUTION 22
EMAIL ETIQUETTE

Whatever advice you give, be brief.
Horace

Most office communication takes place via email or instant messaging (IM). These forms of communication have the advantage of instant delivery, and an ongoing exchange of emails feels more like conversation than correspondence. But you should never be tempted to use email to shield you from interacting personally with your employees.

it is not unusual for managers to exchange several hundred emails a day

EFFECTIVE EMAILS

The same guidelines for effective paper communication apply in the paperless environment of the email.

Always fill in the subject line This makes it easy for the recipient to see at a glance what your message is about.

Avoid email shorthand Always use full, grammatically correct sentences.

Keep your comments brief and to the point without being terse If what you have to say requires more than a few paragraphs, consider making a phone call instead.

Review before you send Once you hit 'send', the message is gone. If you wouldn't write something in a letter or a memo, don't write it in an email message either.

Remember, deleted email can still be recalled That offhand comment you fire off in response to a question about someone's performance could return to haunt you months or years from now.

Check the recipient line before sending With distribution lists and bulk forwarding, the message you send to your superior 'for your eyes only' could end up on hundreds of other computers.

SOLUTION 23
ESTABLISH THE STANDARDS OF ACCEPTABILITY

'Do not go where the path my lead, go instead where there is no path and leave a trail.'
Ralph Waldo Emerson

Just as parents need to set limits and structure at home, managers need to establish boundaries and organization for their employees at work. As a manager, it is your job to tell employees what they can and cannot do. When you are wearing your parent hat, you are reinforcing core values and the behaviours that support them.

managers sometimes must explicitly describe what is and isn't appropriate for employees to wear, say and do

THE EFFECTIVE MANAGER

When you are functioning effectively in your manager-as-parent role, your employees can be expected to:

- Know and follow established guidelines and procedures.
- Understand that there are clear and consistent consequences for stepping outside the boundaries.

Just as you might have to tell your 10-year-old son to stop spitting out the car window, you might need to tell a 32-year-old administrative assistant that she can't swear on the telephone or a 50-year-old sales representative that he can't shave during the morning staff meeting. Sometimes people push limits just to be sure those limits are still in place.

- Accept accountability for meeting project timelines rather than blaming others if things go wrong.
- Be comfortable in coming to you with problems or concerns.
- Respect you, but not fear you.

THE INEFFECTIVE MANAGER

Your employees are adults, and they have adult rights and responsibilities. They have been hired to perform specific tasks and accomplish particular goals. You might be wearing your parent hat too long if:

> *if you want people to act responsibly, you have to give them responsibility – and hold them accountable for meeting it*

- You look at the employees sitting in your office airing yet another dispute and realize that if they were younger and shorter, they'd be telling tales.
- 'Nobody told me I had to do that' is a familiar chorus in staff meetings.
- Employees ask permission to go to the toilet or to take a break.
- No assignment gets completed without repeated visits to your office to be sure it's being done right.
- You have to make excuses to your superiors when your employees fail to complete projects either on time or correctly.

QUICK FIX: MODEL BEHAVIOUR

Meetings are one place in which managers can model the behaviour they want to see in their department. Employees will notice whom you acknowledge and how you acknowledge them. They watch how new ideas are accepted or cut off, and whether the established feedback loop is functional or merely lip service. See Solutions 17 and 18 for how to run meetings effectively.

SOLUTION 24
LET THEM MEET IF THEY HAVE TO

Be not afraid of going slowly, be afraid only of standing still.'
Chinese proverb

Meetings have become a way of life. There are staff meetings at work, PTA meetings, meetings for social organizations, and even family meetings. Yet, at a conservative estimate, over half the time spent in meetings is unproductive and inconsequential. There are some good reasons to have meetings, but there are often better reasons to avoid them. As a manager, you must separate the two and support the productive meetings while trying to eliminate the unproductive ones.

you're battling the social condition for meetings, and it may take some time to nudge others out of the almost physical urge for a get-together

YOURS IS NOT THE ONLY VIEW THAT COUNTS

Your employees may think meetings are good to some degree and upper management may see meetings as proof of productivity. In the beginning, be judicious and cut as many meetings as possible. Be realistic and know a meeting may be necessary for many reasons, including, at times, because someone else insists on having one. Take it slowly and work to lower the number over time.

BAD REASONS FOR MEETINGS

Job justification Meetings satisfy a need people have to visibly justify what they do for their pay.

Poor leadership When people make decisions collectively, they are safe from individual responsibility and blame.

Lack of focus Activity is often so scattered that multiple people from around the organization must agree to a course of action.

Vying for power Meetings have become a modern jousting field for power and control.

Habit People have developed the habit of having meetings.

QUICK FIX: IS A MEETING NECESSARY?

It makes sense to meet if two or more people need to know the same information, or if staff need to know different pieces of information about the same topic. However, if two or more people need to know different things, a meeting is likely to be ineffective: an individual is likely to switch off for the facts that don't relate to her, and so they may not be paying attention for the information that does.

SOLUTION 25
DECODING BODY LANGUAGE

'I speak two languages, Body and English.'
Mae West

More than half of all communication is conveyed in our body language, the unspoken messages that our posture and gestures convey.

Body language often reflects subconscious messages, the content of communication that escapes the intellect's control and manipulation. In other words, your body doesn't always tell the same story as your words. Understanding this can be a powerful tool in reinforcing the messages you give your team and in hearing what they have to say to you.

IDENTIFY THE WARNING SIGNS

An employee may be saying one thing, but his body language may reveal a different message. Without knowing it, he will disclose what he is really feeling if you know what to look out for:

The manager's eyes wander to the computer screen rather than focusing on the person in front of him. His arms cross and his foot starts to jiggle. His words say: 'You did a great job with the presentation. I've had phone calls from several people saying how much they enjoyed it.' But his body says: 'Will she never leave? I have a conference call in ten minutes, and I have to finish the budget report by 4...' The account executive sitting across from him hears she's doing a great job, but his body language is sending out different signals.

Feet dragging Implies lethargy.
Head down Suggests timidity.
Shoulders drooped A sign of weariness.
Slovenly posture May no longer care.
Shifty eyes and fidgeting May indicate nervousness.
Arms crossed on chest A defensive stance.
Hands in pockets He may be hiding something from you.

QUICK FIX: POSITIVE MESSAGES

You can greatly improve the consistency between your words and your body language. Here are a few tips:

WHAT YOU SAY
'I think you are doing a great job.'

WHAT YOU SHOULD DO
Maintain eye contact It's okay to look away now and then; this is not a stare-down.

'I want to hear how I can help you.'

Open your posture If seated, let your arms rest on the chair arms; if standing, let them hang naturally at your sides.

'I want to know how you would tackle this task.'

Sit alongside Sitting directly opposite can be confrontational.

'I'm interested in what you have to say.'

Don't play with your hair, jewellery, pen It's important to be engaged.

SOLUTION 26
BE A GOOD LISTENER

'The spoken word belongs half to him who speaks, and half to him who listens.'
French proverb

Too many people view listening as a passive act when it's actually just as active as talking. The problem is that we tend to spend listening time thinking about what we're going to cook for dinner tonight, or whether those concert tickets are still available, or just about anything else but what the other person is saying.

listening is an activity that requires a full and focused attention.

When an employee crosses her arms across her chest before she speaks and says, in a tense, high-pitched voice, 'Yes, I'd be happy to research that information', what is she really telling you? That she has enough work already without taking on more? That she's cold and wishes she'd brought her cardigan to the meeting? That she can't stand the database librarian she'll have to contact to request the information? You can't know without asking further questions, but you do know there's more to her answer than the words she's said.

FOCUS YOUR ATTENTION

Effective listening is an activity that requires your full and focused attention:

- Engage your mind to slow down your brain; let it hear every word.
- Don't let your attention wander; most listening mistakes occur when you switch off.
- Don't cross the line from anticipation to assumption; assuming will almost always get you in trouble.
- Maintain and keep eye contact; this shows that you're listening and helps you pick up on non-verbal cues.
- Don't formulate your response while the person is still speaking; you can't be listening to someone else if you're listening to yourself.

QUICK FIX: CLEAR COMMUNICATION

Here are two great tips for helping your employee to get their thoughts across to you:

Ask open-ended questions Don't close down a potential discussion by framing questions in such a way that you limit how someone might respond. A question that requires a yes or no response can stop conversation faster than walking out of the room. With open-ended answers, you can keep asking questions, and the conversation continues.

Listen and repeat Paraphrase what you hear in response to your questions to be sure that you actually understand what your employee is telling you.

SOLUTION 27
GIVE EFFECTIVE FEEDBACK TO EMPLOYEES

'Use soft words and hard arguments.'
English proverb

People constantly seek feedback from their managers. Some ask for it directly: 'How did I do?' Others are less direct: 'What did the client say?' Be generous and consistent with feedback and recognition.

we want to know what others think of us; it helps us to develop a sense of belonging, accomplishment and confidence

It may be a good idea to hold a team meeting at the end of the week to recognize work completed and to discuss problems and challenges. Employees are held accountable before their peers, and, more importantly, they have the opportunity to shine in front of their colleagues. Give credit to everyone who participates in bringing a project to completion, and compliment teamwork.

POSITIVE FEEDBACK

When a manager says, 'I have some feedback for you,' employees often hear, 'Let me tell you how you screwed up – again!' Feedback is best given often and in small bites. In fact, when feedback becomes a communication loop, most people don't notice that it's even taking place. Instead of waiting until an assignment is completed to congratulate or critique the employee's performance, offer compliments and suggestions along the way. Offer congratulations on a report well written or a project completed ahead of schedule. This individual attention shows that you notice and care about individual effort.

SOLUTION 28
ENCOURAGE FEEDBACK FROM YOUR EMPLOYEES

'Examine what is said, not him who speaks'
Arabian saying

As a manager, you need to let your superiors know when there are problems. Who knows better what improvements need to be made than the people who do the work? It makes good business sense to listen to what your staff have to say. Employees who feel there is no audience for their concerns can become frustrated.

Successful companies create working environments in which employees and managers feel welcome to share their views and concerns.

regularly hear what your employees have to say, and make the lessons learned available to all

When companies begin involving employees in identifying problems and designing solutions, there is a dramatic leap in buy-in. Once employees feel they are owners in the process, they become enthusiastic supporters of improvement efforts.

SCHEDULED FEEDBACK

Make time to regularly hear feedback from team members. Using open-ended questions, ask about their experiences and how they see their accomplishments interacting with the bigger picture. Stress that this is not a secret performance evaluation, and bring up your own concerns about where things might be going off track. If people can see problems developing, it's better to take steps while it's still possible to do so rather than burying your head in the sand.

SOLUTION 29
DON'T MAKE PROMISES YOU CAN'T KEEP

'It is better to keep your mouth closed and let people think you are a fool than to open it and remove all doubt.'

Mark Twain

When you are managing a team, it's your role to establish clear boundaries and expectations. If you have decision-making authority, let employees know what they might influence and what

can't be changed. Don't set expectations that you can't meet; it damages your credibility.

Take care not to give employees the impression that they have a voice in everything. If they do, provide structured, efficient ways for them to share their opinions and suggestions. If they don't, giving them the illusion that they do will only lead to frustration and resentment.

RECOGNIZE THE LIMITS OF YOUR AUTHORITY

Many nice-guy managers prefer for their employees to feel that their contributions matter, but sometimes decisions are made irrespective of the employees' feelings; it is better to recognize this from the outset than build unrealistic expectations.

Do not ask your team for their input when you know that none of the suggestions they make will be acted upon. If a decision is beyond your control, admit it. You can still give your employees an opportunity to voice their thoughts and concerns, but do not be afraid to admit that you may not have the authority to act on their suggestions.

ADVOCATE WHEN NECESSARY

There will be times, of course, when you need to become an advocate for your employees.

This may take the form of going to your boss and saying, 'We're really overworking this team. We have to give them some relief before they break down and we lose momentum.' Advocacy is about getting support to help meet personal and company goals, not letting people run away from their responsibilities.

THE MANAGER'S DILEMMA

Your challenge is to balance the needs of the organization, the demands of customers and clients, and the desires of employees. To be consistent and effective in supporting a company's principles, managers must also be committed to them. You must feel that you can and do use them as the guiding force in your interactions with employees. If you deeply resent certain corporate policies or goals, commitment will be difficult for you. Ask yourself:

- What is it, precisely, that I don't like?
- Why do I feel so strongly about it?
- Do other managers share my feelings?
- Could I live with this policy or goal if I understood the reason for it?

If you feel your concerns have merit, you have a duty to report back to upper management.

SOLUTION 30
BE SENSITIVE TO FRICTION

'Argument is the worst sort of conversation.'
Jonathan Swift

The workplace forces people into relationships with each other that otherwise might not exist, and while they will most often get along just fine, sometimes there will be problems. It's important for you to always have your finger on the pulse of your team so you immediately know when things are out of sorts. As soon as you realize that something isn't right, it's important to take action straight away.

when people interact, conflict is inevitable, maybe not today or tomorrow, but eventually

GET INVOLVED

Employees expect managers to 'protect' them, and to watch out for them. When this doesn't happen, employees grow resentful and frustrated; morale slides, taking productivity with it. Sometimes the issues that drive employees away seem minor, yet they reflect an underlying problem with trust and betrayal.

When personalities clash, tension can disrupt teamwork and productivity. Be proactive; avoid conflict by building in a structure that helps employees work together. But, in the meantime, keep a lookout for the warning signs, which may include:

- Uncomfortable silences at the beginning of meetings.
- Bitchy gossiping in the staff room.
- Unnecessary competition between team members.

- Complaints about individuals dropped into feedback sessions.
- People being left out of department social events.
- Colleagues hiding from each other by building book or pot plant 'screens'.

RESOLVING CONFLICTS

The way you deal with conflict will depend on the personalities involved; but be sure, the worse thing you can do is nothing at all. Put on your parent, mediator and cheerleader hats. You need to take decisive action and at the same time help individuals see each other's perspectives – without taking sides yourself, of course (see Solution 53). If reasoning with them doesn't work, you may need to consider separating them either temporarily or permanently. Forcing people to co-operate with each other can backfire. Don't jeopardize other team relationships and the integrity of a project by trying to engineer the impossible.

QUICK FIX: CREATING A GOOD ATMOSPHERE

You can foster good working relations by setting a good example. Here are some common practices to instill in the workplace:

Be cheerful Welcome your staff with a cheery 'Good morning' every day and mean it.

Be friendly Take the time to find out what your staff like to do in their spare time.

Be polite Always say thank you when work is delivered on time.

Be respectful Don't assume that an employee can work late just because you can.

Be kind Try making your assistant a cup of coffee for a change.

SUMMARY: PART THREE
GET HEARD AND LISTEN

21   **Rallying the troops** Motivate your staff and keep them performing to the best of their abilities.

22   **Email etiquette** Apply the same rules for effective paper communication to the paperless environment of the email.

23   **Establish the standards of acceptability** It is your job to tell employees what they can and cannot do.

24   **Let them meet if they have to** Support the productive meetings but eliminate the unproductive ones.

25   **Decoding body language** Learn to read the unspoken messages a person's posture and gestures convey.

26 **Be a good listener** Listening is an activity that requires your full and focused attention.

27 **Give effective feedback to employees** Help your staff to develop a sense of belonging, accomplishment and confidence.

28 **Encourage feedback from your employees** Create a working environment in which your staff are able to share their views and concerns.

29 **Don't make promises you can't keep** Let employees know what they might influence and what can't be changed.

30 **Be sensitive to friction** When people interact, conflict is inevitable eventually.

NOTES

part
four

part
four

LOOK TO THE FUTURE

SOLUTION 31
ONE SIZE DOES NOT FIT ALL

*'Remember always that you not only have
the right to be an individual, you have
an obligation to be one.'*
Eleanor Roosevelt

Some people require constant direction, feedback
and redirection. Others are better left to a general
framework within which they are free to structure the
job's tasks and measure of progress. As a manager
of individuals, you need to consider how
each employee works most productively, and then shape your overview and
interactions to be appropriate with the
employee's work style.

*meet with employees
one on one, so you can
gauge just how much
structure each needs*

THE NEED FOR STRUCTURE

Some employees do not function well in
an environment with minimal structure.
They may not know how to channel
their energy into productive tasks with
measurable outcomes. Employees who
need a lot of structure need a manager
who is willing to be more hands-on (see
Solution 32). Those employees for whom
structure is important tend to:

A key challenge for a
manager whose personal
work style is structured is
letting go to let others find
their own way – but let
go you must. Employees
will rebel if they feel that
you have a 'my way or
no way' approach.

- Be tidy and organized.
- Arrive and leave on time at the same time every day.

- Follow routines.
- Meet deadlines without fail.
- Appear disciplined and goal-oriented.
- Keep to the rules.

DEALING WITH THE CREATIVE THINKER

Channelling creativity into productivity can be a significant challenge for a manager. At times, the creative individual can appear to have little regard for authority, rules, structure and routine. Here are some ideas for stimulating and supporting the creative thinker:

Present assignments in general terms Explain the desired end result but allow her to find her own way there.

Factor in time for mistakes Trying new things may take longer, but it's critical to take risks sometimes, to explore new ways of doing things.

Resist the temptation to be critical Shooting down ideas is the surest way to kill creative thinking.

no company can thrive or survive without fresh ideas

QUICK FIX: STIMULATING CREATIVITY

Many managers are tempted to stay with tried-and-true methods, but be wary of this: familiarity breeds repetition, and this may lead to complacency and stagnation. Consider sponsoring workshops conducted by outside resources. Creative people are always looking to broaden their base of knowledge and expertise, and new faces bring fresh perspectives. Employees are sometimes more willing to question and raise issues with outsiders than they are with internal trainers or consultants.

SOLUTION 32
PROVIDE STRUCTURE

'Remember that you are needed. There is at least one important work to be done that will not be done unless you do it.'
Charles L. Allen

The backbone of structure is clear communication. Employees need to know what they are expected to do and by when. They need to be clear about their priorities – what is more important and what is less important – and what they should do when tasks compete for their time and resources. As a manager, your role is to help employees establish priorities and processes to support them.

when people don't know their priorities, what gets completed is often frustratingly trivial, and the important stuff gets left undone or missed completely

A HANDS-ON APPROACH
If necessary, meet with the employee daily and take them through exactly what it is you require of them.
Be specific Identify the tasks that must be accomplished by the end of the day.
Be smart Make sure the employee has the necessary tools to complete the tasks and that he knows how to use them.
Troubleshoot Identify common problems

Managers need to be willing to revise and adapt. What an employee self-monitors and what the manager monitors should evolve over time. It should be the manager's aim to play a less direct role in sculpting the employee's daily activities.

that might arise, and establish a procedure for dealing with them.
Follow up Meet with the employee at the end of the day to discuss how he approached the tasks and what actually got finished.
Evaluate Discuss expectations, and review what worked and what didn't, so that you have something to build on the following day.

it can be useful for new team members to devise a workflow chart that outlines priorities and procedures

STEP BACK SLOWLY

Establish procedures for identifying and addressing emergencies and unexpected changes in priorities. At first, this might require that the employee come to you whenever work deviates from the planned schedule. As the employee becomes more skilled in structuring and adjusting priorities, the procedures might shift to general guidelines for when to contact you and when to proceed without assistance. Over time, and as the employee's confidence grows, designate daily tasks as part of their routine, and make them responsible for these with less monitoring from you.

QUICK FIX: MONITORING PROGRESS

The key to success is brevity and regularity. Here are a few ideas for providing feedback and reinforcement:
- Desk stop – visit each employee at their workstation at the same time each day.
- Daily or weekly progress reports – get individuals to provide you with a one-page summary.
- Standing meeting – hold a quick department meeting at the end of each day.

SOLUTION 33
GET THE JOB DONE

'The superior man is firm in the right way, and not merely firm.'
Confucius

Every job has specific, core tasks as well as general responsibilities, as defined by the job description. Most jobs require interactions among employees to generate the products or services that are the company's reason for existing. While the job description outlines the framework, it is the manager's role to establish the criteria for completing the specified tasks, and to monitor and assess an employee's performance by a process of evaluation.

While formal evaluation meetings (appraisals) are likely to take place twice a year (see Solution 38), as a manager you are responsible for ensuring that employees fulfil their obligations and commitments on a day-to-day basis.

> *'No' may be an overwhelmed employee's cry for help, a last-ditch effort to stem the flow of work before she drowns completely*

> Be respectful. Recognize that any additional tasks you ask an employee to undertake are optional so that she feels she can say no should she still choose to (but the chances are she won't).

HELPING EMPLOYEES DEVELOP AND REACH THEIR POTENTIAL

People are most likely to accept and comply with performance standards if they have a role in establishing them. Work with them to establish their short- and long-term personal goals. Help them to identify their strengths, where those strengths can take them, and how they might change or improve their options by taking certain training courses or learning special skills. For more on this, see Solution 39.

employment is a negotiation that starts and ends with an employee's ability to meet the needs of the company

QUICK FIX: DEALING WITH NO

Most employees welcome the opportunity to stretch themselves beyond their everyday tasks on occasion, so long as they don't feel that they are being taken advantage of. It can be annoying to hear an employee say, 'That's not in my job description,' but it may be possible to turn it around:

Meet privately Ask, non-confrontationally, why she feels this way, taking time to listen to her concerns; perhaps she is resentful that others are not pulling their weight.

Explain the reasons Assure her you respect and value the contributions she is already making and that you wouldn't ask her to do more unless you needed her help and had confidence in her abilities.

Offload tasks See if there are some aspects of her job that can be delegated to another employee to help her take on the assignment you need her for; identify the benefits to her of taking on the additional responsibilities.

SOLUTION 34
BUILD AN EFFECTIVE TEAM

'Coming together is a beginning. Keeping together is progress. Working together is success.'
Henry Ford

By bringing employees together to form a team you can help them to work more effectively to solve problems and achieve their collective goals. As a manager, it is your job to put together the right team of people for the job.

a manager must establish the right type of team and recruit the right people for the right reasons

TYPES OF TEAM

There are many different types of team and each has different requirements for the manager:

Standing team Works towards goals that are ongoing; usually a very stable group, but keeping individuals motivated and connected to the task can be difficult.

Ad hoc team Assembles to achieve a particular goal and then disbands; often has representatives from different parts of an organization; can be dynamic but you may not have direct involvement in the team's recruitment.

Departmental team Forms around job responsibilities; familiarity can help the group to gel, but the range of experience may be limited.

Cross-functional team Forms with employees from different parts of an organization; there will be a breadth of knowledge but decision-making generally is more dispersed, as the people on the team all report to different managers.

TEAM ROLES

To get the most from your team you need to make sure that the team members you recruit bring the right mix of personal qualities to provide the group with the psychological boosts they need to keep interacting effectively:

take into account what the team needs and try to find the round peg that fits the round hole

The cheerleader Always there to boost morale, has natural enthusiasm, and can help to motivate the team; may be difficult to deal with on Monday mornings.

The devil's advocate Focuses on the heart of the problem and seeks accountability in all situations; can be perceived to be argumentative.

The muse Brings the creative spark and inspires others to think outside the box; depends on others to turn those bright ideas into actions.

The counsellor Brings experience and wisdom, and provides unique insight into solving problems; values everyone's opinion.

The facilitator Gets the job done; organization and delegation are strengths, but may be overbearing and controlling.

QUICK FIX: RECRUITING THE RIGHT PEOPLE
Involve others in the team; pay attention to their impressions – if a new person doesn't mesh well, teamwork will be difficult.

SOLUTION 35
GET YOUR TEAM WHAT IT NEEDS TO SUCCEED

'In the middle of difficulty lies opportunity.'
Albert Einstein

Even the most self-sufficient, effective work teams can't function in a vacuum. They need you, and sometimes other departments or work groups, to provide the resources required to achieve their goals. They need the proper equipment and supplies, an appropriate work space, adequate administrative support, and suitable environmental amenities. It is your role as manager to make sure all of these elements are in place.

who wouldn't want to go the extra mile for a manager who at least tries to go the extra mile for them?

You must do everything within your power to get the very best for your team so that they can achieve their very best.

LET THEM GET ON WITH IT

If you want people to act responsibly, you have to give them responsibility – and hold them accountable for meeting the goals you set them. As long as they have the necessary knowledge, tools and resources to complete their assignments, your team members may work best when you give them the space to make their own decisions. Make sure they understand what you expect from them and when you expect it, then let them get on with it. But be ready to serve as facilitator, mediator, teacher, mentor, cheerleader, coach and parent – whatever they need.

> *when people interact, conflict is inevitable; it may not happen today or tomorrow, but eventually team members will clash*

MANAGING CONFLICT

Sometimes people simply don't get along with each other. Although we like to believe that adults can put aside their differences to work towards common goals, this doesn't always happen. However, there is a difference between true conflict that threatens progress and the everyday tensions that adults must learn to manage. Don't move in quickly at every sign of trouble. The ability of team members to work through their differences to renewed understanding and co-operation is crucial to the group's success. There will be squalls and occasional storms, but conflict is a normal part of human interaction.

QUICK FIX: DEALING WITH PROBLEMS
Involve team members in the resolution of problems to increase their co-operation. If they help to create the solution, the more they have invested in making the agreed-upon changes work. Find a common objective and brainstorm possible solutions, and select the solution that has the best chance of meeting everyone's needs.

SOLUTION 36
SHARE YOUR POWER BUT STAY IN CONTROL

'If I have seen further, it is by standing on the shoulders of giants.'
Sir Isaac Newton

When others take on tasks and accountability on your behalf, you divide the work among many willing hands, and progress can occur more quickly. For this to be effective, you need to establish two aspects of power-sharing: first, empower employees to make decisions and second, delegate responsibility to them. By extending authority and responsibility to your employees, you deputize them so they take over a task or project on your behalf while still being answerable to you.

ARE YOU READY TO SHARE?

Many managers give responsibility without the necessary corresponding authority. It's like putting people into a kitchen and asking them to prepare a meal, only not letting them use any of the pots and pans, knives or ingredients. It's time to empower and delegate more if you answer yes to one or more of the following questions:

- Do you have more than eight people reporting directly to you?
- Do you rarely include other team members when trying to solve problems?
- Do people have little say in how they perform their duties?
- Do you find yourself constantly thinking, 'I should have done this myself'?

empowerment:
giving people the authority to make decisions and do things on your behalf without seeking permission

SOLUTION 37
HAVE CONFIDENCE IN YOUR TEAM

'Ah, but a man's reach should exceed his grasp, or what's a heaven for?'
Robert Browning

Your success as a manager is dependent on engaging the potential of everyone on your team. You must be able to recognize the value that each employee can bring. Everyone will have different strengths and weaknesses, but each can play a crucial role. First, and perhaps most importantly, you need to show your staff that you believe in them.

show the members of your team that you trust them to take on jobs and make the decisions necessary

BUILD THEIR SELF-BELIEF

You may need to help your employees develop their self-assurance. The quickest way to show them that you believe in their ability is to give them responsibility. Start with small goals, and help them to succeed by coaching and mentoring along the way. As their confidence grows, build their responsibilities. Avoid the temptation to direct, command and micro-manage.

Hand off some power, see positive results, and then try more.

Watch some children – even at play, they are daring and willing to create worlds and imagine themselves with tremendous abilities and futures. It is only as adults that many people find themselves limited; people often lack self-confidence because circumstances have conditioned them to believe that nothing is possible.

SOLUTION 38
MAKE TIME FOR
PERFORMANCE EVALUATION

'Feedback is the breakfast of champions.'
Popular saying

Most companies have a structure for evaluating job performance, and formal reviews between manager and employee are set at regular intervals. Sometimes this is referred to as the appraisal process. A traditional structure may feature an annual review, usually on the anniversary of the employee's start date, with supplementary quarterly meetings.

the annual performance review is an opportunity to step back from the day-to-day tasks and to see the bigger picture

The performance evaluation is an opportunity to review whether an employee is achieving the goals, expectations and standards that have been set for them, and a chance to identify goals, expectations and standards for the next review period. At its best it is a two-way discussion and should be embraced by both parties, not feared and resented.

360-degree feedback: a performance review approach in which managers collect feedback about an employee's job performance from others who interact with the employee

DON'T SAVE IT UP

Regular communication – daily or at least weekly – is the most effective way to both monitor and shape employee performance. It remains your most effective tool as a manager. Don't save things, good or bad, for a formal evaluation meeting. Nothing you or the employee says in a formal meeting should come as a surprise to either one of you.

KEYS TO A SUCCESSFUL APPRAISAL

The appraisal process can be a meaningful tool in the career development of your employees if done well. Setting goals for your employees, monitoring their performance, and finding ways to coach, support and counsel are all things that an appraisal should achieve. Here are some tips for having a good one:

- Review employee files in advance and speak to other members of staff with whom they have worked for 360-degree feedback.
- Bring a clear written agenda of what you want to cover to the meeting.
- Have documentation to hand for any issues to be discussed but keep it discreetly in a file folder.
- Schedule plenty of time to address any questions or concerns that arise.
- Take notes and encourage them to do the same.
- Present problems directly and objectively, and have a general idea of how they can be resolved.
- Don't focus only on the improvements employees need to make; give equal weight to their talents and contributions, and recognize growth and development that has taken place.
- Give employees a chance to talk; listen without interrupting, and ask questions only after they have finished speaking.
- If follow-up is necessary, make sure timelines are agreed before the meeting ends.

SOLUTION 39
HOLD ON TO GOOD PEOPLE

'The sharp employ the sharp.'
Douglas William Jerrold

Your company entrusts you with its employees – its most valuable resource – and it expects you to help them to develop their skills. If you don't want to lose your staff to the competition, you need to support them and help them to grow.

give your employees opportunities to grow and develop new skills

By taking the time to develop your staff and keep them engaged and fulfilled, you will reduce staff turnover; as your employees grow, they will be able to take on more responsibilities, so freeing you up to do the same.

TRAINING FOR ALL

Every now and then, if your budget allows, let employees attend workshops that aren't directly related to their jobs but that interest them. A technician, for example, might enjoy a class in graphic design, or a sales representative might like to go to a seminar on construction methods. Some choices might seem a bit far removed from their day job, but most people will choose options that align with their longer-term goals.

staff

turnover:
the rate at
which people
leave an organiza-
tion and must be
replaced

INVEST IN YOUR STAFF

You need to be able to show employees
that you can help them to meet their own
goals while achieving the company's goals.
It often doesn't require that much for you to
provide the opportunities your employees want
and need to feel that they are growing
in their role. Use regular feedback to
help employees improve their skills and
performance, and to find out how you
might be able to facilitate their development. Ideas could include:

*on average, people have
three to five different careers
and work for a dozen or
more companies from the
time they enter the workforce
until the time they leave it*

- Asking employees with particular proficiency in certain areas
  to conduct short workshops for other employees.
- Sponsoring lunch-time training sessions in which experts
  from other parts of the company or outside sources conduct
  short presentations.
- Establishing a mentoring programme in which employees pair
  up to learn from each other.

QUICK FIX: STAFF TRAINING

If employees are worth keeping, it's worth your time and energy to
find solutions that will work for both sides. To find out what your
employees need, you could create a departmental training
committee so employees themselves can assess training needs
and present ideas for meeting them.

SOLUTION 40
DON'T FORGET ABOUT YOU

*'Leadership and learning are indispensable
to each other.'*
John F. Kennedy

When you're involved in guiding the careers of others, it's easy to overlook the continuing need to monitor and direct the course of your own. It's still a good idea for you to develop some skill strengths in areas that will continue to be important across the board in business. Learn the basics about the key tasks of employees who report to you so you understand their contributions and how each piece fits into the whole. This also helps you to delegate more effectively and to monitor progress using measures that are relevant and appropriate.

*if your only strength is
your people skills, you
may be left behind if
changes happen*

STAY CONNECTED

As a manager, you make decisions that affect people, projects and productivity. While you are probably not an expert in every function or task that the employees in your department perform, you should have considerable expertise in the key functions that are your department's responsibilities.

STAY SHARP AS A MANAGER

Of course, it is possible for a manager's core skills to be in management. Some people who excel in directing and mentoring may not have core skills in the areas they supervise. If you are such a manager, make sure you keep up to date with the latest management theories, principles and practices.

Many companies will pay, or reimburse, you for costs related to keeping your skills current or learning new skills that are relevant to your job

MAINTAIN YOUR CORE SKILLS

There are many ways to keep your core skills honed. If you are a working manager, you have daily exposure to the changes taking place in your profession. Pay attention to these changes, even if it seems they don't affect you directly. At a minimum, you should:

Enrol in workshops or classes offered Large companies often have training departments that develop and deliver classes to teach customer service skills, quality improvement methodologies, computer and technology skills, and other subjects relevant to the needs of the company's employees.

Maintain active membership in relevant professional organizations Go to meetings, conferences and workshops. Network and build relationships with people who work for other companies.

Take higher education courses It's always to your advantage to stay abreast of current developments in your career field.

SUMMARY: PART FOUR LOOK TO THE FUTURE

31   **One size does not fit all** Adapt the way you interact with each employee to accommodate their individual work styles.

32   **Provide structure** Help employees to establish priorities and processes to support them.

33   **Get the job done** Ensure your employees fulfil their work obligations and commitments on a day-to-day basis.

34   **Build an effective team** Establish the right type of team and bring together the right mix of people for the right reasons.

35   **Get your team what it needs to succeed** Do everything within your power to get the very best resources for your team so that they can achieve their very best.

36   **Share your power but stay in control** Extend authority and responsibility to your employees, but make them answerable to you.

37   **Have confidence in your team** Show you employees that you trust them to take on jobs and make the decisions necessary for success.

38   **Make time for performance evaluation** Set formal reviews at regular intervals, and use these as an opportunity to step back from the day-to-day tasks and see the bigger picture.

39   **Hold on to good people** If you don't want to lose your staff to the competition, support them and help them to develop their skills.

40   **Don't forget about you** When you are involved in guiding the careers of others, it's easy to overlook your own.

NOTES

part
five

part
five

BE AN INSPIRATION

SOLUTION 41
GET PEOPLE TO DO WHAT YOU WANT

'Motivation is the art of getting people to do what you want them to do because they want to do it.'
Dwight D. Eisenhower

The task that faces you as manager is to get people to willingly take on a job and to see it through to its conclusion. Excitement helps at the beginning of a project, but the initial rush of enthusiasm usually wanes as your team starts to experience difficulties; some people are able to keep themselves forging ahead, but most can't, and that's where you need to step in.

people are motivated when they connect what they do to a sense of why they do it

You need to provide your workforce with the reason to take on a task in the first place and to continue to motivate them until the job is completed.

PROVIDING FOCUS

The receipt of a payslip at the end of each month may be the reason your staff come to work, but it is not the reason they take on tasks with enthusiasm and determination. This only happens when you provide them with meaning for

Recognition is important to everyone. In a recent poll, 62 per cent of people who reported dissatisfaction with their jobs also said they felt that their managers failed to recognize and appreciate their efforts and accomplishments. The most effective managers have a word of praise for each employee, every day.

their actions. When your staff connect to the task, understand the reason for it, and can relate it to the bigger picture, they are more likely to fulfil what is expected of them.

HELP YOUR STAFF CONNECT TO THE TASK

To get people to focus on what you need, you have to focus on what they need, which is a connection to something greater. There is nothing more compelling than a sense of purpose and meaning. Simply ordering people to do what they should won't help; in fact, all it is likely to achieve is a feeling of resentment. Meaning is a personal experience, and the reasons to take on a goal that resonate with one member of staff will leave another cold. Some, for example, might be motivated by a challenge, while others may be defeated by a task clearly out of their comfort zone. You need to pay attention to your team members, understand what makes them tick, and get a sense of what draws and what repels them.

QUICK FIX: GET STUCK IN

If you want to motivate others, you need to show them that you are prepared to go the extra distance too. When your staff is up against it, pitch in and help out, and don't ever complain about it.

SOLUTION 42
LET THEM MAKE MISTAKES

'Tell me and I'll remember for an hour; show me and I'll remember for a day; but let me do it and I'll remember for ever.'
Chinese saying

By giving up control to your employees your chances for success are greatly enhanced, but then again so is the possibility for error. As they grow and develop, it is inevitable that your employees will err on occasion; your responsibility as their manager is to help them learn from their mistakes, and to encourage them to carry on in spite of them.

mistakes are the ultimate teacher

DEAL WITH IT

You must accept that mistakes are necessary on the path to learning, and focus on minimizing their effect. Start your employee on smaller projects that have a greater chance of success. As they gain experience, you can increase the complexity of responsibility and the difficulty of the assignment. Throughout it all, make sure you praise and encourage your employees' efforts, irrespective of their success (see Solution 44).

CRITICAL FEEDBACK

Feedback is a great way to help employees improve and grow their skills. Here are some tips and suggestions for the best way to give it:

Deliver the good *and* the bad Some 'good guy' managers give only positive feedback, but when praise is always forthcoming, its value is diminished.

Don't try to sugarcoat the bad When feedback that was initially positive is followed by a contradictory message, it has little value; if the news is bad, just deliver it.

Give feedback regularly and often It becomes a natural element of the work environment, rather than something to be feared.

Criticize privately When less-than-positive feedback involves just one or two people, deliver it individually and in private.

Praise in public To reinforce the team's value, praise the entire work group for its collective efforts; this reminds people that teamwork is about performance, not personalities.

QUICK FIX: REAP THE BENEFIT

Although delegation can, initially, increase the chances for mistakes, an often-overlooked benefit is that it lets managers learn from their employees. The person to whom you delegate a task or project will undoubtedly approach the work differently than you would have, and their approach may even be better.

SOLUTION 43
BRING OUT THE BEST IN OTHERS

'Never tell people how to do things. Tell them what to do and they will surprise you with their ingenuity.'
General George S. Patton

The other roles you adopt as a manager tend to focus on each individual's needs and capabilities. The role of coach, however, requires you to bring together people of diverse skill levels and backgrounds to work as a unified team, to better meet the company's goals.

managers who are good coaches inspire loyalty and respect

EFFECTIVE COACHING

To be an effective coach you must:

Provide timely and specific feedback Give positive comments as soon as possible and say exactly what was good about the work they did.

Establish standards Set goals that are high enough to make employees stretch, but not so high that they're impossible to reach.

Tell the truth Do it with kindness and caring, but always be straight-talking.

Offer suggestions Share ideas for improvement but resist telling employees exactly how to do things.

QUICK FIX: COACHING IN ACTION
The most effective way to become a good coach is to watch a good coach in action. If your workplace is lacking in such role models, take a walk down to your local sports field at the weekend. You'll see good coaches, bad coaches and mediocre coaches, and you'll see how their teams respond to their methods.

SOLUTION 44
CELEBRATE ACHIEVEMENT

'He only profits from praise who values criticism.'
Heinrich Heine

One of the best ways to keep your staff motivated is to foster a working environment in which successes are celebrated – not at the end of the year, the end of the quarter, the end of the month or the week, but each and every day.

SAYING THANK YOU
There are lots of ways to say thank you for a job well done, both big and small. Here are a few ideas:

An annual recognition programme Invite the staff to make nominations for who should be recognized for their contributions.

A departmental dinner Arrange a special occasion to celebrate an outstanding performance.

Time off Send them home early on a Friday afternoon.

Group praise Gather them together on the department floor to celebrate the team's achievements, and bring cake.

Personal thanks Stop by their desk and acknowledge how they have helped you to do your job better.

QUICK FIX: CELEBRATE FAILURES
This may sound mad, but if anything, it is even more important to offer praise when things go wrong than it is when things are going right. When employees fail, it doesn't mean that they didn't try their best, so reward the effort they put in. This way, they will be motivated to try even harder next time around.

SOLUTION 45
LEAD BY EXAMPLE

'Neglect mending a small fault, and
'twill soon be a great one.'
Benjamin Franklin

It is important for you to set the example you want your employees to follow. If you are a workaholic, most of them will be, too. It's fine if you don't have a life beyond work – that's your choice – but you must make sure that you do not establish this as the norm. Your employees are entitled to their personal lives, and unless you encourage them to look for and maintain a work/life balance, you risk them leaving or burning out.

*no one should feel that
their job owns them*

In a recent poll, 44 per cent of those surveyed considered themselves workaholics, to the extent that work activities interfered with or prevented a life beyond their job. More than half of those who worked full-time said they put in more than 40 hours a week.

Encourage your employees to take breaks during the working day, to leave on time most days, and to have periods of extended time off to recharge their batteries. This is good for the employee, and it's good for the company.

CORPORATE CULTURE OR INDIVIDUAL PERSONALITY?

There are always going to be occasions when it is necessary to work late – to meet a tight deadline or to finish a crucial presentation. But if you or your employees are regularly putting in over 40 hours a week, there may be trouble brewing. People who are committed to their professions may enjoy spending more time at work, but then again people who are overburdened may feel compelled to stay late, even though they know the attempt to catch up will ultimately be futile.

HELPING A WORKAHOLIC EMPLOYEE

If you have an employee who regularly burns the midnight oil, try to find out the reasons why. If you don't know the problem, you can't help to find the solution. Give them the chance they need to talk through any problems they might have in a one-to-one meeting:

- Do they have too much work to do?
- Are they making the most efficient use of their time?
- Do they need help prioritizing tasks?
- Do they need any training to help them complete tasks more efficiently?
- Are there problems at home that make staying at work more inviting?
- What can you do to help?

Be supportive and non-judgemental, yet firm. Make it clear that while you appreciate and respect such dedication, no one is expected to work all the time.

QUICK FIX: LEAVE ON TIME TODAY
Take out a piece of paper and write, 'Today I will leave work at 5pm.' Sign it and stick it on your desk where you can see it. Keep your contract with yourself. At 5pm, pack your bag and head out the door. And make sure you let your employees see you do so.

SOLUTION 46
HOW TO BE A TRUSTED GUIDE

'To be able to lead others, a man must be willing to go forward alone.'
Harry Truman

Mentoring is an important role for any manager. It extends beyond teaching in that it relies on establishing a relatively long-term relationship that revolves around sharing and mutual respect. A mentor shares knowledge as well as wisdom – a fine line, perhaps, but a crucial distinction. While knowledge can be learned, wisdom must be acquired.

Knowledge is having the right words; wisdom is knowing when and how to say them – and when to keep them to yourself.

mentoring involves learning on the job, being guided by experienced managers wise in the ways of the company

The original Mentor is a character in Homer's epic poem *'The Odyssey'*, who is charged to look after the family of his close friend Odysseus, King of Ithaca, while he is away at war. On the king's imprisonment, the goddess Athena takes over Mentor's body to help him guide the king's son to safeguard the kingdom. Mentor makes an appearance in many other Greek myths, often as a disguise for a helpful god or goddess.

WHAT DOES A MENTOR DO?

Today's mentors are ordinary people who have achieved extraordinary success helping others reach their goals. Most mentoring is unofficial, though some large companies have structured mentoring programmes to groom potential upper-level managers and executives. More typically, a person with expertise takes interest in a subordinate's career and helps him to:

- Set long-term goals and short-term objectives.
- Explore new directions to achieve goals.
- Identify personal strengths and weaknesses.
- Find ways to develop and grow.

QUICK FIX: SHADOWING

Shadowing is a time-efficient mentoring technique where you put an employee in a situation where he can observe your actions without participating in them. He might sit in on a conference call or a sales meeting, for example, or read and discuss a report you've written, or accompany you to an event where you are giving a presentation. These observed sessions can often be far more effective than any tutored lessons and by observing you in action he will see how you learn from your mistakes as well as your successes.

SOLUTION 47
BE READY TO TEACH

'A master can tell you what he expects of you. A teacher, though, awakens your own expectations.'
Patricia Neal

As a manager it will sometimes be necessary for you to take on the role of teacher, to instruct employees in the expert knowledge they need to do their job to the best of their ability, sharing your skills and knowledge with others so that they can achieve their best results.

A good teacher – one whose students learn – improves both the individual and the company. But it isn't always easy to find a balance between 'Let me show you' and 'Get out of the way, I'll do it myself!'

IF THEY DON'T KNOW WHAT TO DO, SHOW THEM

If an employee is failing to fulfil the essential functions of her job, you may need to step in and show her what to do. Although it can be frustrating when someone cannot do the job that they were hired to do, in the long run it will be a better use of your time to teach them the skills they require, rather than wasting hours correcting their errors.

IT MAY NOT BE EASY

Not all situations end in success, of course. Some employees will resist the suggestion that they need to clean up rusty skills or learn new ones. Some managers will lose patience when improvements fail to be immediate and dramatic. Some managers will know what they want from their employees but don't know how to express their needs in ways that their employees understand.

essential functions: the primary tasks and responsibilities of a job that an employee must be able to perform

QUICK FIX: FIND A TEACHER

If the role of teacher doesn't come naturally to you, consider finding another way to fulfil this expectation (as your budget allows):

- Hire consultants to conduct workshops or seminars for your work group or department.
- Send employees on external training courses.
- Encourage employees to take evening/weekend classes that directly improve their job skills and reimburse them for the cost.
- Find other member of the organization who can share their expertise.

SOLUTION 48
MANAGE YOUR TIME EFFECTIVELY

'Time is what we want most, but what we use worst.'
William Penn

With so many others depending on you, your ability to manage your time effectively will spell the difference between success and failure for you, your staff and ultimately the company. You need to stay on top of what you are doing, and this requires establishing a good framework in which to work.

THE BASIC PRINCIPLES

Set priorities There are never enough people, hours or funds to do everything you would like in the time you have, so you must make sure you get the important things done first.

Establish the plan Set up systems to track what needs to be done, the order of completion, and who is responsible for what. This ensures people do not duplicate efforts and no one waits for what they need.

Schedule accurately Build flexibility in so that when things go wrong, you'll have the ability to recover and put things right.

Delegate duties You can't do everything yourself; delegate key tasks and give your staff the authority to do the things you require of them.

Review often Communicate with your staff on a daily basis to make sure things are running as planned.

Change direction if necessary Be ready to modify your plans as situations and circumstances demand.

Improve constantly Always be on the lookout for ways that you can improve the overall effort or organization.

SOLUTION 49
PROMOTE GOOD COMMUNICATION

'There's no use talking about the problem unless you talk about the solution.'
Betty William

Good communication encourages creative interaction among all members of your team. Your communication strategy should support, encourage and reinforce your goals. Develop healthy habits and encourage them among your staff too.

IT'S NOT WHAT YOU SAY, IT'S THE WAY THAT YOU SAY IT

Be positive Avoid criticism where you can; focus on what can be done to improve situations rather than simply pointing out what is wrong.

Have fun Be upbeat and enthusiastic whenever possible. The more your audience enjoys listening to you, the more information they will retain.

Be open Communication is a two-way activity, so you need to be receptive to what others have to say.

Have respect Hear the person out before responding. Even if you disagree with their point of view, you must show that you value their contribution.

if you have nothing good to say, it may be best to say nothing at all

QUICK FIX: BE RESPECTFUL
You set an example for the culture of communication among your team. Always bear this in mind and never:

- Criticize upper management.
- Gossip about other managers.
- Slag off individuals in the team.
- Complain about customers.

SOLUTION 50
MAKE A GOOD IMPRESSION AT MEETINGS

'When you meet a man, you judge him by his clothes; when you leave, you judge him by his heart.'
Russian proverb

As a manager you are likely to spend a good deal of your working day in a meeting of one sort or another. Present yourself to the best of your ability, and make sure that the behaviour of others mirrors your impeccable good manners.

PRESENTING YOURSELF

You might be the most interesting person in one-to-one situations yet transform into a bumbling mumbler in a group setting when all eyes and ears are focused on you. You need to relax and be yourself. Here are a few tips for speaking in front of a group:

- Talk at a moderate pace – not too fast, not too slow.
- Form your words clearly and cleanly.
- Vary the tone and pitch of your voice.
- A little movement can add interest, but don't let your gestures become too distracting.

THE CONDUCT OF OTHERS

The way you allow others to conduct themselves at meetings that are run by you provides your employees with an insight into your values and managerial qualities. If they are allowed to run rampant with total disregard to the opinions of others or to the agenda, the manager may be considered a bit of a wimp. A well-structured and well-run meeting is an indication of an organized and disciplined manager. You should:

- Create an atmosphere of openness.
- Demand a respectful attitude towards others.
- Encourage input from everyone, including the quieter members of staff.

For more specific advice on running an effective meeting, see Solution 18.

IT'S A MEETING, NOT AN INQUISITION

If an employee is being bombarded with questions or criticism, step in to put an end to it. If employees see that those who stick out their necks end up getting them chopped off, they are unlikely to be willing to speak up themselves, even when the topic concerns them. There is a balance between open dialogue and abuse, and it's your role to maintain it and to protect employees who present unpopular perspectives.

QUICK FIX: PERFECT PRESENTATIONS
As the saying goes, 'practice makes perfect.' Here are a few ideas for perfecting your skills:

- Change the outgoing message on your voicemail daily; strive for a different tone each day.
- Give your presentation in front of a mirror.
- Videotape yourself and play it back after the meeting.
- Take a workshop or class in public speaking training.

SUMMARY: PART FIVE
BE AN INSPIRATION

41   **Get people to do what you want** Motivate your staff to take on a task and see it through to its conclusion.

42   **Let them make mistakes** Help your team to learn from their mistakes and to carry on in spite of them.

43   **Bring out the best in others** Managers who are good coaches inspire loyalty and respect.

44   **Celebrate achievement** Foster a working environment in which effort and success is celebrated daily.

45   **Lead by example** Look for and maintain a work/life balance for yourself and for your staff.

46 **Be a trusted guide** Help others to achieve their career goals by giving them the benefit of your experience.

47 **Be ready to teach** Make sure your staff have the skills and knowledge they need to do their job to the best of their ability.

48 **Manage your time effectively** Stay on top of what you are doing and establish a good framework in which to work.

49 **Promote good communication** An effective communication strategy should support, encourage and reinforce goals.

50 **Make a good impression at meetings** Present yourself to the best of your ability, and make sure that others mirror your behaviour.

NOTES

part
six

part six

TACKLE THE TOUGH STUFF

SOLUTION 51
DRAW THE LINE

*'The true way to render ourselves happy is
to love our work and find in it our pleasure.'*
Françoise de Motteville

One benefit of having a job is social interaction. However, when friendships at work interfere with employee productivity, you have a problem that needs to be addressed. It is possible, and desirable, to set reasonable standards for socializing in the workplace.

APPROPRIATE SOCIAL INTERACTIONS IN THE WORKPLACE

Here are some ways you can moderate workplace socialization:

- Encourage friendly and supportive socializing; set the tone in your dealings with employees.
- Discourage gossip and the spread of rumours.
- Support collaborative efforts among employees on projects that warrant more than one participant.
- Encourage employees to consult one another, to share knowledge and expertise.
- Provide opportunities for staff to talk, such as when the workday begins or for a few minutes before meetings start.

QUICK FIX: SET AN EXAMPLE

Model an appropriate balance between socializing and working in your own behaviour. If your employees see you standing in the doorway chatting about the guy in the accounts department who's dating the chairman's daughter, they will believe it's okay for them to do the same thing. Your actions speak louder than words.

SOLUTION 52
DEALING WITH CLIQUES

'The worst solitude is to be destitute of sincere friendship.'
Francis Bacon

clique:
a small group that forms around specific interests and excludes those who do not share those interests

Sometimes what starts as friendship can develop into a clique whose members exclude rather than welcome others. This is a problem when these alliances shut out other team members and prevent them from doing their job efficiently.

DON'T IGNORE IT

You have a duty to intervene when you notice that:

- Employees spend more time socializing than working.
- A group keeps individuals from being successful by undermining their efforts.
- A clique keeps information from others to make themselves look better.
- Rumours and gossip abound.

don't hide in your office or pretend you don't know what's going on

QUICK FIX: COLLABORATION

Cliques can form when two teams join forces. Foster a more inclusive mix by splitting the team into smaller working groups and assign each one different projects.

SOLUTION 53
DEALING WITH DISAGREEMENTS

*'People who fight fire with fire usually
end up with ashes.'*
Abigail Van Buren

It is impossible to get on with everyone
all the time. A little conflict between team
members need not necessarily be a bad

*some people mix about
as well as oil and water*

thing and could be refocused into a competitiveness that can spur each
on to greater achievement. However, disagreements can be counter-
productive when individuals are constantly at each other's throats.

WEAR YOUR MEDIATOR HAT

Telling people to stop having a problem does little good. When
team members find it difficult to agree, it is your responsibility to help
them find a way to resolve their differences. Reaching an agreement
doesn't necessarily mean that each side gets what it wants. Sometimes solutions are collaborative (all parties gain) and sometimes
they involve compromise (all parties give something up). However,
each side must feel satisfied with the solution, or the conflict remains.
Mediation is most effective when you aim to:

- Focus on common goals and look for common ground to help
  you reach those goals.
- Treat all parties, and their viewpoints, with respect.
- Propose win-win solutions.
- Remain interested but impartial.

mediate:
to intervene to
settle a dispute
between two
parties

- Establish a process for assessing the
  success of the agreed-upon solutions.

RESOLVING CONFLICTS

Co-workers don't have to be good friends; they just
have to find ways of working with and around each other. If you are
going to help people to negotiate their differences, you need both
sides to establish:

A shared allegiance When both sides want to achieve the same
outcomes, they're often more willing to search for common ground.

Mutual respect Respect is the foundation for trust; people must
respect each other before they can trust one another to fulfil the
agreements they reach.

Open minds Each party must be willing to both talk and listen so
that together they can explore possible solutions.

Willingness to change Obviously each individual believes that his
or her perspective is valid and correct. After listening to each other
and discussing the problems, both must be willing to change their
positions to accommodate suggested solutions.

QUICK FIX: STRONG PERSONALITIES

Disagreements often occur when there are strong personalities on
the team. You could try:

- Assigning them to different aspects of the team's goals.
- Separating them physically if the work space allows you to.
- Temporarily swapping one with an individual from another team.

SOLUTION 54
DEALING WITH THEIR ANGER

'How much more grievous are the consequences of anger than the causes of it.'
Marcus Aurelius

The workplace can be a frustrating environment and sometimes employee frustrations are channelled into inappropriate outbursts of anger. People get angry when they feel afraid, sad, threatened, insecure, disappointed – when things are out of their control. Anger elicits a response when other efforts fail to do so, and that can give an individual a false sense of control.

> *anger is an unmistakable sign that a person has exceeded her tolerance for a situation or behaviour*

WHAT SHOULD YOU DO?

An angry outburst can frighten not only those who witness it, but the person who is ranting and raving too. To help an employee regain control:

Intercede immediately Do not allow matters to become even more volatile.

Remove the audience If she has her outburst in front of other staff, take her into another office, or ask the other employees to leave.

Separate the behaviour from the person and request that the behaviour change immediately Look away to give her a few moments to compose herself, but stay in the room if safe to do so; this indicates your willingness to help.

Be an active listener Let her explain her position; don't assume you already know what the problem is. Ask any questions you may have only once she has finished.

Ask what solutions the employee would like to see If the suggestions make sense, discuss how best to implement changes; if they don't, explain why, and offer an alternative.

Reiterate any agreements and establish a follow-up plan This formalizes the discussion.

ESTABLISH THE UNDERLYING REASONS

The actual event that sends an employee over the edge is often something minor that may not be related to the real reasons for their anger. To manage the situation, you need to find out what the underlying reasons are:

- Have they been overlooked for promotion?
- Are they being taken for granted?
- Do they have too much work to do?
- Do they feel unsupported and unappreciated?

QUICK FIX: GET THEM OUT OF THERE

Meetings are forums for the expression of different ideas and concerns, and when people feel strongly about things, tempers can flare. When someone bursts into a rage in front of others, it's nearly impossible for him to back down without losing face. By removing an angry person from a group situation you often remove the need for him to continue raging, and give him the opportunity he needs to regain his composure and dignity.

SOLUTION 55
DEALING WITH YOUR ANGER

'He who angers you conquers you.'
Elizabeth Kenny

Angry managers are just as much a problem in the workplace as angry employees. When you blow a gasket, your employees can make a convenient scapegoat for your anger. Sometimes, of course, they are the reason you are frustrated in the first place, but just as often you may be letting off steam because of frustrations at home. Whatever the cause, an angry outburst is never the right response.

don't blow up at an employee just because they are in the wrong place at the wrong time saying the wrong thing

ANALYZE YOUR ANGER
When you find yourself getting angry at an employee, take a deep breath and ask yourself:
- Is this employee the source of my anger?
- If not, who or what is?
- If so, why?
- Can I talk to them about this without losing my cool?

If the answer to that final question is no, cool down before taking action (see Solution 56 for some tips). Before approaching the employee, outline some notes that explain the problem as you see it, the consequences of the problem, and the solutions you propose. Stick to this 'script' in your conversation with your employee to keep calm and focused.

SOLUTION 56
DON'T LET IT GET TO YOU

*'When you come to the end of your rope,
tie a knot and hang on.'*
Franklin D. Roosevelt

As a manager you have to deal with the needs of your employees on the one hand and the demands of the company on the other, which can all too easily result in stress. A certain level of stress is not necessarily a bad thing – it can keep you motivated and interested. It's all about balance. Learn to recognize the symptoms of too much stress, and take action before you lose control.

SYMPTOMS OF STRESS
You may be exhibiting symptoms of stress if you:
- Feel anxious about things you can't change.
- Are unable to get to sleep or wake up in the middle of the night worrying about things not done.
- Lose your temper.
- Have no interest in the activities you normally enjoy.

QUICK FIX: LETTING OFF STEAM
When things get too much, take time out to relieve the stress:
- Count to 10 before responding to an irritating question; it will save you apologizing later for an off-the-cuff response.
- Close your office door and take 5 minutes to calm down; try some deep-breathing exercises.
- Go for a 10-minute walk to clear your head.
- Book a few days' leave – they will survive without you.

SOLUTION 57
DEALING WITH CONSISTENT UNDERPERFORMERS

'Ninety-nine percent of the failures come from people who have the habit of making excuses.'
George Washington Carver

Employees represent a significant investment on the part of the company; when problems occur with their productivity, you must try to resolve the situation to protect this investment. Look out for problem behaviours (see Solution 58) and help your employees to improve.

HOW TO HELP
Whatever the reason for an employee's lack of productivity, don't ignore their failings. Do not make excuses for them, or be tempted to take over from them. Employees need you to offer guidance on how to do things correctly, efficiently and in keeping with company policies.

consistent, regular feedback is the most effective way to keep most employees on the right track

THE RIGHT WAY TO HELP
When working with a struggling employee, it's important to establish a few basics:

Make sure help is wanted Establish that the employee is willing to comply with efforts to improve his performance.

Establish goals and priorities and clear steps for meeting them Ensure he understands how not achieving these will affect the work of his colleagues.

Monitor progress Review and address any problems that he has experienced in completing goals.

Work towards independence Make self-monitoring his long-term aim.

DO YOU HAVE A PROBLEM?

Take the following test to see if you have an employee who is flailing and failing. How often do you find yourself:

Taking time out of your day to redo what an employee has done?
☐ Never   ☐ Once or twice a week   ☐ Daily

Redoing the same tasks for the same employee over and over again?
☐ Never   ☐ Once or twice a week   ☐ Daily

Spending time after hours on work tasks that aren't really yours?
☐ Never   ☐ Once or twice a week   ☐ Daily

Waking up at night worrying whether a project will be completed on time?
☐ Never   ☐ Once or twice a week   ☐ Daily

Defending an employee's work to other team members, your superiors or clients?
☐ Never   ☐ Once or twice a week   ☐ Daily

Asking other employees to pick up extra work to cover for an employee who isn't pulling their weight?
☐ Never   ☐ Once or twice a week   ☐ Daily

If you ticked the 'Once or twice a week' box more than three times, you should take action.

SOLUTION 58
DEALING WITH THE DISSATISFIED EMPLOYEE

'I would rather try to persuade a man to go along, because once I have persuaded him, he will stick.'
Dwight D. Eisenhower

Sometimes your employees will feel unfairly treated. They may not understand why they have been overlooked for promotion, or they may feel that they are being asked to do much more than their colleagues for less pay.

> *recognize the contributions of all team members from the star players to the backroom staff*

Whatever the reason for their dissatisfaction, your staff need to know that they can come to you to air their concerns – whenever they feel they need to, not just when you determine it is appropriate for them to do so. Anything less, and you risk grievances and resentment taking hold.

PROBLEM BEHAVIOURS

When employees feel unable to express their frustrations by bringing their problems to you, they may let you know in more subtle ways. Tell-tale signs that things are not as they should be include:

- Missed deadlines.
- A negative attitude.
- Angry outbursts.
- Unhelpfulness.
- Stirring up trouble with other employees.

- Showing up late, leaving early or taking excessively long lunches.
- Flagrantly violating or ignoring company policies.

WHEN PEOPLE FEEL HARD DONE BY

When an employee comes to you with an accusation of unfairness, it is important to address it completely and thoroughly. Focus on the employee who is complaining: it is not your responsibility to defend your actions regarding other employees, and revealing too much information can result in complaints about the breaching of confidentiality.

PASSED OVER FOR PROMOTION

If the employee has applied for a job in another department and has been disappointed, make sure you find out all the facts before scheduling a meeting to discuss the situation. Failing to do so is like scuba diving without checking the air gauge on the tank – it won't be long before you're in serious trouble.

Ask the employee about his goals – with your department, with the company, with his career. Where would he like to be in three, five and ten years' time? How does he see his current job leading to the fulfillment of his long-term goals? If you can, structure a formal improvement plan that supports those goals, with the employee's full participation.

> Do not slack on disciplinary matters. When an employee puts you to the test by violating company policy, ethical standards, or even laws, you must take prompt and appropriate action. Failing to do so at the very least diminishes your authority within your work group and at worst may make you complicit in the violation.

SOLUTION 59
MANAGING RESTRUCTURING AND DOWNSIZING

'Time changes everything except something within us which is always surprised by change.'
Thomas Hardy

Companies restructure or downsize to conserve resources and cut expenses; these are necessary measures to help them stay profitable and competitive

doing more with less is both your challenge and your goal

when marketplace conditions alter. Some jobs may be merged into one and others may disappear altogether. As a manager, you need to prepare your employees for these changes, and you must support the company by making those changes work.

TREAT EVERYONE FAIRLY

At no other time are you likely to feel more in the middle than now: it is your role to carry out upper management's intentions and plans, even though you might feel your first loyalty is to the employees who report to you. As much as you would like to sneak in a few hints or even make a few midnight phone calls to certain employees to give them

restructuring: a company's re-organization of its operations to function more efficiently and competitively

a heads-up, you must not. If you know about coming changes, you must keep the knowledge to yourself unless it is your role to announce it to your department.

HELPING THEM TO COME TO TERMS WITH CHANGE

There's nothing easy about hearing that the world you've become accustomed to has suddenly changed through no fault of your own, but the way you communicate change can greatly affect the way your employees deal with it.

Deliver the news individually This is just as important whether the person is staying or leaving; although a group announcement might be easier for you, it could be very difficult for people who react emotionally to the news.

Be sensitive to leavers' wishes Some employees may want a leaving party, others may prefer to go without a lot of attention; let the individual decide and respect her wishes.

Support those who remain Meet with surviving employees to explain what has happened and why. Allow them to express their feelings: they may feel angry that friends are now out of a job and guilty that they still have theirs.

Welcome newcomers If your department is gaining new staff as a result of restructuring, you need to explain to your existing employees why, when other people have been let go of, others are being taken on. New staff members should not have to deal with others' resentment.

Communicate responsibilities Be sensitive to issues of workflow, personality conflicts, confusion over who does what, and any other potential problems.

SOLUTION 60
WHAT TO DO WHEN IT HAPPENS TO YOU

'Change is the law of life. And those who look only to
the past or present are certain to miss the future.'
John F. Kennedy

Major changes in your company will
undoubtedly lead you to reconsider your
own career. You may have to move to
another department within the company;
in fact, you may need to move to another
company altogether. Often, when departments are restructured,
managers are among the first to go.

*if you don't believe in
the company's new
direction, make sure
you are equipped to
move on*

A company cannot guarantee to provide you with job security for
life; while they may expect loyalty, you owe it to yourself to be ready to
make a move when circumstances make it necessary to do so.

ALWAYS BE PREPARED FOR THE WORST

Just as you can't warn your employees of impending change, upper
management cannot give you advance notice that your job may
be at risk. Therefore, it is always a good idea to be prepared for this
eventuality. Keep your professional skills current and stay abreast of
technological advances, both in your field and in general. Keep an
eye on the job market in your area of expertise, just in case you do
find yourself on the seeking end of the job hunt.

READY FOR CHANGE

Here are some ways you can be prepared for whatever changes might come your way:

Keep your CV up to date Review and revise your CV on a regular six-monthly basis so that it reflects any training that you have had, new responsibilities you have taken on, major projects you have completed, and key successes you have achieved.

Network at every opportunity Collect business cards from people you meet at professional gatherings and even at social events.

Polish your skills and experience Take on any training opportunities that would enable you to translate your talents into positions in other areas of work.

Volunteer In addition to the personal satisfaction you will gain from fulfilling needs within your community, this will help you to further expand on your skills and extend the network of people you know.

Build a financial buffer Set aside a small amount from your salary each month – as little as 2 to 5 per cent can quickly add up to a tidy emergency fund; aim for a figure that will carry you through three to six months of unemployment.

QUICK FIX: THE RIGHT CONNECTIONS

Make it a point once a week to call, have coffee with, or go to lunch with, someone you know who works for another company that employs people who do what you do.

SUMMARY: PART SIX
TACKLE THE TOUGH STUFF

51   **Draw the line** Set reasonable standards for socializing in the workplace; work should be fun but not so much so that no work gets done.

52   **Dealing with cliques** You must intervene when alliances shut out other team members and prevent them from doing their job.

53   **Dealing with disagreements** Mediate to find ways to help your employees to resolve their differences.

54   **Dealing with their anger** Take control and find out the underlying reasons for the outburst.

55   **Dealing with your anger** Whatever the cause, an angry outburst is never the right response; keep calm and focused at all times.

NOTES

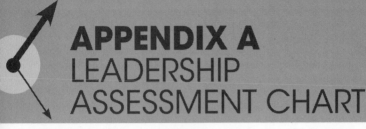

APPENDIX A
LEADERSHIP
ASSESSMENT CHART

This assessment is designed to provide you with a personal profile of your leadership competencies, attitudes and behaviours. Give yourself 4 points if you answer 'Frequently', 2 points if you answer 'Sometimes', and 0 points if you choose 'Rarely or Never'. Total your score when you finish to determine your leadership rating.

SECTION A ACTIVISM/CHANGE	FREQUENTLY	SOMETIMES	RARELY	NEVER
1 When I sense that something is not right at work or in the community, I find a way to make it better.	☐	☐	☐	☐
2 I understand who in my organization can help me or my employer achieve our goals.	☐	☐	☐	☐
3 I have little tolerance when inertia overcomes a project or employee.	☐	☐	☐	☐
4 I respect the past and our company's legacy; however, I do not avoid rethinking 'tradition'.	☐	☐	☐	☐
5 I am committed to quality.	☐	☐	☐	☐
6 I am driven towards high performance.	☐	☐	☐	☐

SECTION B INTELLIGENCE/LEARNING				
1 I believe that I have the mental capacity to think through most complex situations.	☐	☐	☐	☐
2 I welcome the challenge of complex issues and problems.	☐	☐	☐	☐
3 I am committed to creating an environment where mistakes become learning experiences.	☐	☐	☐	☐
4 I encourage my staff to disagree with me.	☐	☐	☐	☐
5 I tend to hire people who have talents, knowledge and skills I don't possess.	☐	☐	☐	☐

	FREQUENTLY	SOMETIMES	RARELY	NEVER
6 I believe I am more intelligent than lucky.	☐	☐	☐	☐
7 I am not intimidated by ingenious people.	☐	☐	☐	☐
8 I like being around 'smart' people.	☐	☐	☐	☐

SECTION C VISION

	FREQUENTLY	SOMETIMES	RARELY	NEVER
1 I look at things around me and I am able to envision how they can and will be better.	☐	☐	☐	☐
2 I articulate abstract ideas to others quite easily.	☐	☐	☐	☐
3 I have a picture of the future that I am committed to fulfilling.	☐	☐	☐	☐
4 The vision I have for the organization incorporates what is strongest about the firm.	☐	☐	☐	☐
5 I often utilize symbols and images to motivate my employees.	☐	☐	☐	☐
6 I communicate and exemplify high standards of performance.	☐	☐	☐	☐

SECTION D ALTRUISM/CARING

	FREQUENTLY	SOMETIMES	RARELY	NEVER
1 I generally respect my co-workers.	☐	☐	☐	☐
2 I hold general conversations with my employees.	☐	☐	☐	☐
3 I genuinely admire and appreciate the people who work with me.	☐	☐	☐	☐
4 Knowing about my employees' values is important to me.	☐	☐	☐	☐
5 Knowing about my employees' hobbies is important to me.	☐	☐	☐	☐
6 I encourage employees to help each other develop to their full potential.	☐	☐	☐	☐
7 I communicate often with employees about work.	☐	☐	☐	☐
8 I communicate often with my employees about leisure activities.	☐	☐	☐	☐
9 I provide personal attention to people who may need it.	☐	☐	☐	☐

SECTION E COMMUNICATION

	FREQUENTLY	SOMETIMES	RARELY	NEVER
1 I am generous in my praise and recognition of my employees who perform quality work.	☐	☐	☐	☐
2 I seek the opinions of my employees.	☐	☐	☐	☐

SECTION F FLEXIBILITY

	FREQUENTLY	SOMETIMES	RARELY	NEVER
1 If plans go sour, I recover easily and without searching for a scapegoat.	☐	☐	☐	☐
2 I have a high tolerance for ambiguity.	☐	☐	☐	☐
3 When an employee has a 'bright idea' I try to find a way to accommodate it.	☐	☐	☐	☐

SECTION G SPIRIT/SOUL

1 I have an inner sense of balance that allows me to move through the day with serenity.	☐	☐	☐	☐
2 I know how to relax.	☐	☐	☐	☐
3 I take the time to enjoy the non-work component of my life.	☐	☐	☐	☐
4 I have an emerging leadership style that is truly my own.	☐	☐	☐	☐
5 I know how to 'play'.	☐	☐	☐	☐
6 I allow my employees to see and experience all facets of my personality.	☐	☐	☐	☐

SECTION H INTEGRITY/EGO STRENGTH

1 I do my own 'dirty work'.	☐	☐	☐	☐
2 I don't disappear when an employee is in trouble.	☐	☐	☐	☐
3 I don't ask anyone to do something I would not do.	☐	☐	☐	☐
4 If I had to choose I would treat employees better than bosses.	☐	☐	☐	☐
5 I admit or explain when I am wrong.	☐	☐	☐	☐
6 I can and do take the heat.	☐	☐	☐	☐
7 I consider myself a symbol of success.	☐	☐	☐	☐
8 I am comfortable with who I am.	☐	☐	☐	☐

SECTION I CREATIVITY/INNOVATION

1 Ideas come readily to me.	☐	☐	☐	☐
2 I strive to have employees conceptualize old problems in new ways.	☐	☐	☐	☐
3 I provide new ways of looking at issues that may seem puzzling to employees.	☐	☐	☐	☐

SECTION J RELIABILITY

	FREQUENTLY	SOMETIMES	RARELY	NEVER
1 I ensure that my employees have the information and resources necessary to do the job.	☐	☐	☐	☐
2 If I say it is so, I make it so.	☐	☐	☐	☐
3 I don't avoid problems or sticky issues.	☐	☐	☐	☐
4 I make sure that there is congruence between what employees are asked to do and what they can expect from me in support of their efforts.	☐	☐	☐	☐

SCORING

Now add up your total score.

Frequently _____ **Sometimes** _____
Rarely _____ **Never** _____
TOTAL _____

200+ You are well on your way to being a good manager. The attributes and behaviours you exhibit tend to motivate, enrich, educate and inspire others.

150–199 You are working well towards becoming a good manager. By examining the various factors of the assessment, you can see where you need to focus your attention and even reflect on your assumptions about work, the people who work with you and why you want to manage. Consider how you can stimulate more accountability and independence in others by showing more vulnerability within yourself.

110–149 Your reasons for attaining the position of manager may be more self-centred than organizationally based. Trust is an essential component, and your score indicates that either you believe that the people you work with are not trustworthy or you doubt your own ability to manage. Either way, you may be holding on too closely or not delegating at all. Consequently, those around you may not be confident of your support. Examine why you are so dedicated to 'control' and what you really have to lose by guiding rather than forcing.

0–109 You may have been too long under the influence of managers who do not value the employee's fundamental need to do well and to be appreciated. You have a lot to learn. Pursue new mentoring relationships within the organization, take some management courses, read recently published management books, and gain the experience to become an effective manager.

APPENDIX B
REFLECTIVE LEADERSHIP EVALUATION TOOL

This evaluation helps you obtain feedback from the people you manage to get a better understanding of your effectiveness. Give copies to your employees and ask them to complete the questions. To tally your score, give 4 points for answers of 'Frequently'; 2 for answers of 'Sometimes', and 0 points for 'Rarely or Never'.

	FREQUENTLY	SOMETIMES	RARELY	NEVER
PART I COMMUNICATION				
1 Do you feel that you are kept informed and are not 'in the dark' about your job?				
(a) Are you aware of priorities?	☐	☐	☐	☐
(b) Are you clear about expectations?	☐	☐	☐	☐
(c) Are you sure of responsibilities?	☐	☐	☐	☐
(d) Are you clear about timeframe and deadlines?	☐	☐	☐	☐
2 Do you feel that you receive adequate acknowledgement of and recognition for your contributions?	☐	☐	☐	☐
PART II COACHING				
1 When you are having difficulty with a task, do you receive:				
Support?	☐	☐	☐	☐
Direction?	☐	☐	☐	☐
Feedback?	☐	☐	☐	☐
2 When you are given a new responsibility, do you receive:				
Support?	☐	☐	☐	☐
Direction?	☐	☐	☐	☐
Feedback?	☐	☐	☐	☐
3 Are you involved in setting your own performance goals?	☐	☐	☐	☐

PART III CONTINUOUS TRAINING

	FREQUENTLY	SOMETIMES	RARELY	NEVER
1 Do you feel that you have all the necessary skills and competencies to perform your job?	☐	☐	☐	☐
2 When you are given a new task or responsibility, do you receive adequate training?	☐	☐	☐	☐
3 Are you given opportunities to learn, grow and develop to expand your career options?	☐	☐	☐	☐

PART IV CREATIVE PROBLEM-SOLVING

	FREQUENTLY	SOMETIMES	RARELY	NEVER
1 Are you given opportunities to:				
(a) Participate in decision-making?	☐	☐	☐	☐
(b) Provide solutions?	☐	☐	☐	☐
2 Are you involved in determining methods and procedures?	☐	☐	☐	☐
3 Do you experience a sense of power and control in your job?	☐	☐	☐	☐

PART V CHALLENGE FREQUENTLY

	FREQUENTLY	SOMETIMES	RARELY	NEVER
1 Do you associate feelings of achievement and satisfaction with your job?	☐	☐	☐	☐
2 Do you feel that your skills and talents are being used to their fullest?	☐	☐	☐	☐
3 Are you comfortable with your level of responsibility?	☐	☐	☐	☐

SCORING

Now add up the number of times you ticked each category.

Frequently _____ **Sometimes** _____
Rarely _____ **Never** _____

HOW MANY TIMES DID YOU TICK 'FREQUENTLY'?

Between 23 and 28 Congratulations; you're doing a great job in creating an environment that fosters motivation in employees. However, there is always room for improvement, so look at the areas where you didn't receive such a high rating.

Between 11 and 22 You're doing a good job but you need to focus on the questions in which you were marked 'Sometimes' or 'Rarely/Never', because they point to areas where you need to set goals and make changes in your behaviour.

Between 0 and 10 You need to change your management style. First, work on the areas where you received the 'Rarely/Never' rating. Then move on to the areas where you received the 'Sometimes' rating.

FURTHER READING

Lundin, Stephen C., PhD, Harry Paul and John Christensen *Fish! A Remarkable Way to Boost Morale and Improve Results* (Hyperion, 2000)

Miller, Marlane *Brainstyles: Change Your Life Without Changing Who You Are* (Simon & Schuster, 1997)

Morgenstern, Julie *Time Management from the Inside Out* (Henry Holt & Company, 2000)

von Oech, Roger, PhD, *A Whack on the Side of the Head: How to Unlock Your Mind for Innovation*, Revised Edition (Warner Books, 1998)

Tannen, Deborah, PhD *Talking from 9 to 5: How Women's and Men's Conversational Styles Affect Who Gets Heard, Who Gets Credit, and What Gets Done at Work* (Harper Paperbacks, 1995)

Tieger, Paul D. and Barbara Barron-Tieger *The Art of Speed-Reading People: Harness the Power of Personality Type and Create What You Want in Business and in Life* (Little, Brown and Company, 1998)

ABOUT THE AUTHORS

Gary McClain, PhD is the director of research at Sachs Communication Group, Inc, a media consulting and research firm. Dr McClain has held positions in companies such as Lockheed Martin and OglivyOne.

Deborah S Romaine is the co-author of more than a dozen books.

Erik Sherman is a writer, entrepreneur and consultant. He has owned several small businesses and served as a business consultant to firms ranging from start-ups to *Fortune* 500 companies. As a journalist, he has long covered business and interviewed major business figures, including the CEOs of ChevronTexaco, Sysco and Kaiser Permanente, on issues of management and leadership.

Eric Yaverbaum heads Ericho Communications, one of the most sought-after virtual agencies in the USA. He has overseen public relations programmes for brands such as American Express, Sony, IKEA and H&M. He previously served as president of Jericho Communications, the eleventh-ranked public relations firm in the country. He is the author of *Leadership Secrets of the World's Most Successful CEOs. PR Weekly* named him one of the heroes of the industry.

INDEX